DARK TIMES CATERING

A MEMOIR

ALEE REINA HOFFMAN

Dear Reader,

The decision to read this book is a decision to embark on an emotional journey, and I am deeply honored you're joining me. Together, we'll navigate the depths of the human experience, encountering both profound highs and lows.

Most of this story unfolds between 2019 and 2021, with some flashbacks to earlier years. For clarity, each chapter begins with the year and location. Some names and identifying details have been changed to protect privacy.

This memoir has an intentional design. While we'll move through some of the darkest and rockiest times I've known, we will ultimately reach a place of light and steadiness. I invite you to hold that reassurance as the story unfolds.

You'll also encounter descriptions of spiritual practices and experiences that may be unfamiliar. I've shared them simply and clearly, so you can step into the narrator's perspective, even if it differs from your own.

The book begins with the version of me who wanted to deny the cracks in a foundation that was about to collapse; the one who wasn't sure if she could get through it all, let alone enjoy life again. But it was written and infused with the energy of the woman I am now—forever changed, yet more integrated than not.

I began writing in November 2021, expecting a much shorter timeline for completion. Instead, the process became a teacher in trusting the natural pace of both healing and creation. The extra time gave me the reflection I needed to become the accurate narrator this story deserved. This version of me has moved through many cycles and continues to find her way. What you'll find here is a passage rebuilt with words and intention, so we can walk it together.

My hope is that in reading my story, you'll come into contact with your *own* tale of resilience. Perhaps a part of your path is ready to be seen in a new light. Maybe you'll allow for more reverence, compassion, and resolution with your own process — or the process of another. You might feel a new connection to your roots and community begin to emerge. And it may be that you hadn't realized you were on a similar ride to the one shared in these pages... until now.

Possibly, you arrive here with the same question I had:

When the time comes, can I really make it through?

This book is for all of us, wherever we are on the map.

I hope *Dark Times Catering* offers what you need, and that you can fully receive whatever drew you here.

May it reconnect you to your own peace, your own levity, and your own spark of inspiration. And most of all, may you discover that when the time comes—and even if the unthinkable happens—you, too, can find your way through.

With sincere gratitude,
Alee
Spring 2025

For Gina, Chuck, and Gabriel

For everyone who's lost something they thought they
couldn't live without

FEBRUARY, 2019: LOS ANGELES, CA

THE MISSING PIECE

I stood on the side of the road and waited until there were no cars in the driveway. I prayed that no one would see me, that the side door would have some give to it, and that it wasn't as dangerous as I'd been told. I would have to be quick.

The beach traffic had finally begun to thin out after the sun dipped behind the ocean, and the bright warm day was giving way to an inky sky and chilled breeze. The loud buzz of live music, clinking plates, and laughter from the waterfront cafés softened into a low hum as folks headed home.

It was a Monday night in February, which meant winter hours

for everyone on this stretch of Venice Beach— except for the lifers at Hinano's posted up on their stools in the cool darkness, oblivious to the rolling waves and sunshine that had been just beyond the sticky floors, pool tables, and ancient popcorn machine.

Finally, it was my turn. I darted across the street, then slowed to a walk as I tucked behind a palm tree and surveyed the best way in. The house was a small two-flat, painted a nondescript beige with the kind of stucco texture that had been popular in the 1970s.

I slipped around the side and gave the heavy back door a good shove until I was inside the small cement patio, where there was a small BBQ grill and a broken surfboard awaiting disposal. A jungle of potted plants filled the rest of the wide first-floor porch.

I held my breath and listened to make sure no one had heard me. Then I craned my neck to check the driveway one more time. Coast still clear. I hoisted myself up onto the railing, careful not to knock anything over. A loud crash and a pile of spilled dirt and roots would definitely draw attention.

The second-story porch was a narrow metal strip with a square view of the ocean. I pulled myself over the railing and carefully inched around the hula hoop and bicycles wedged tightly into place.

Once I was sure no one from the neighboring beach houses could see, I crawled over to the sliding glass door and slipped my hand through the loose screen. Stretching as far as I could, I caught the latch, flicked it up, and after a few tries, the old glass door rumbled open. Finally, I was inside.

I entered into a maze of box fans scattered across the room, blowing air against the torn-up walls. I turned right into the bedroom off the hallway and found a similar situation—walls ripped open, tarps and paint cans covering the floor, and another loud fan buzzing as it strained to dry the wet paint. A long plastic tarp was draped across the bed, but the blanket underneath was still visible. Jet black and screen-printed with stars and crystals.

I had the sudden urge to rip off the tarp and crawl into bed, even for just a minute, but I didn't know how much longer I had before someone showed up. It was time to act quickly: find the jewelry and make my getaway.

It wasn't in the obvious places like the nightstands, jewelry rack or on the dresser. I rifled through drawers, my fingers searching for a balled-up sock with something precious hidden inside. Nothing. I got down on the tarp and squeezed under the bed, shining my phone flashlight into the corners and behind the headboard. Just empty space.

"Fuck!" I hissed. I was sweating now, heart pounding. Where was it? Had it been misplaced—or taken?

The questions suddenly became insurmountable. A cold wave of panic flushed over me, and I began to shudder.

There I was, the day after my thirty-fifth birthday, *breaking into my own apartment*, now condemned due to mold—after months of arguing about it with our landlord. And to top it off, I was casing the joint for my own jewelry, which I'd just realized hadn't made it into my travel bag like I thought. Cool way to start the year.

The plastic tarp squeaked beneath me as I trembled uncontrollably and thought:

I can't get on the plane. I can't pack one more bag. And I might've just lost the most important family heirloom I was ever given.

My phone pinged. It was my friend, Morgan:

> Hi, are you back? Did they figure out repairs with your place?

I could almost hear her feather-soft voice through the text. I looked around at what had once been my sanctuary, wondering if it was even possible to clean out the mold now, especially since my room had been the epicenter of the problem. Maybe that was what had me feeling so frantic.

My mind flashed back to the afternoon when the whole problem began. After weeks of rain, my bedroom wall had sprung a leak, and an arched stream of water had pitched through the air

3

like I was living inside a concrete fountain. I had been in the middle of a session with a new client at the time; a no-nonsense type. I remembered keeping my voice calm and steady, thankful it wasn't a video session, as I slowly slid out of my chair and onto the floor with my laptop.

Reasonable rent on the beach was rare and highly coveted, and I'd quickly learned that our landlord, Mona, wasn't too concerned about upkeep. She could have another eager tenant within a day. Besides that pesky hole in the wall, the apartment had everything I needed. I just wanted it to all go smoothly.

To my relief, Mona had promptly sent over her "work-men." But they turned out to be more like a ragtag group of local surfers. It was hard to tell if they had ever done this kind of job before.

"Oh, easy," one said with a casual grin. "It's just a hole. We'll dry out the wall real good, add some spackle, and paint over it tomorrow morning. You don't even have to leave for this."

As it turns out, we all should have left.

Mold had been growing invisibly since the water damage two and a half years earlier. It had never been dried out properly; not in my room, not in the walls, not in the roof. Over time, the other tenants and I began to connect our mounting health issues— weight gain, headaches, sore throats, fatigue, brain fog, and emotional swings—to potential mold exposure.

Eventually, we insisted that Mona test the place again or we would be calling "the city," as my downstairs neighbor put it in a stern email. Both floors tested positive for dangerously high levels of mold. All residents were evacuated, and finally a real remediation company was brought in to replace the surfer dudes.

Even though we'd suspected something all along, it was still jarring that something invisible had caused so much damage, both inside and around us. Enough to require tearing off the roof.

I texted Morgan back with shaky hands:

IDK. They said two more weeks to finish.
Actually I'm here right now bugging out.
You nearby?

I looked down at the bed again.

Back when it was still my cozy sanctuary, I'd prop myself up with memory foam pillows and gaze out the high square window across from the bed, listening to the waves crash while a breeze drifted in. Although it turned out that I'd been breathing in mycotoxins along with fresh ocean air, it had felt heavenly at the time. Now the window was covered in towels. And I wasn't even supposed to *be* here; banished for the month by Mona while the apartment was undergoing the repairs.

I had rented this room in someone else's apartment when I first moved to L.A from the Midwest. My housemate, Kimiko, was a laid-back woman who worked for an environmental firm in Santa Monica and had an elderly bulldog named Boba. The rest of the space was hers: the furniture, the dishes, the family photos.

I'd spent the summer working from the West Coast, and the plan to officially move here with my boyfriend had just dissolved —along with our relationship and most of what filled our apartment back in Chicago. With little time between the intense breakup, the move, and everything happening with work, I kept it simple: all I needed was a bed and a desk facing the ocean. My life felt stripped down to its essentials, but in that simplicity there was relief.

This space was also where I ran my practice as a spiritually focused teacher and consultant—writing articles, crafting offerings, filming videos, and facilitating sessions with clients around the world. And for the first time in a while, I got to choose just what *I* wanted in a bedroom and bathroom. Many nights I came up the sandy walkway from the beach, filled the tub, and hung my salty swimsuit on the showerhead before submerging myself in a bubble bath—my version of heaven.

When I wasn't working, I had all of Venice Beach at my finger-tips, and a new era of freedom to enjoy. Admitting the relationship had run its course also meant admitting that the desire to move here had really just been mine, and it was time to live it out.

There were daily strolls on the beach, every kind of spiritual event I could have imagined, dates with guys *decidedly* different from those in Chicago, and fun shopping days on Abbot Kinney. Once I found my rhythm, life felt exciting and full here. We hosted big parties for the Venice Canal Christmas Parade, and kept such a variety of beach and BBQ gear on hand that my friends started calling me "Vacation Mom."

Until recently, the hole in the wall had been a distant memory. I had moved in expecting only a temporary respite before finding something else, but it had worked out so well—with Kimiko as my housemate and the epic location of this apartment—that I never left. Life in this neighborhood had felt like a reward for the leap I'd taken. Now, staring at the tarp-covered bed, I wondered if it would ever feel that way again.

Since the remediation started, I'd been bouncing between friends' homes and Airbnbs, trying to stay grounded. But now, two weeks later, I felt especially scattered. Was the brain fog and weepiness worse inside the house? I thought so. But after every-thing else that had gone on this year, it was hard to tell.

When my brother Gabe heard what was happening, he'd suggested I come stay with him in Miami. He had just decided to rent an apartment there after a few work meetings turned into a bigger plan.

"I'm being spontaneous!" he said. "It feels like something *you* would do. And now I can finally do things like this again."

I was happy for him. And it felt good to say yes. To rest into his invitation, to celebrate his new beginning, and to get some time together after a long year of family crises that seemed to finally be winding down.

The last hurdle would be getting on the plane without falling apart. Fifteen minutes later, I walked over to the front door and pulled back the big sign that had been hastily scribbled with:

DO NOT ENTER—

REMEDIATION IN PROGRESS!

Now that I had gotten into the house with no issues, I felt more comfortable having Morgan come through the front. She strode in wearing a chic linen sundress, her glossy brown hair punctuated with straight bangs that framed her light eyes.

"Okay, let's sort this out," she said in her soothing tone, seemingly unfazed by the chaos. I tried to mask my anxiety with a greeting and a smile but took a heaving breath as I looked down at the clothes strewn across the floor.

"Something just *collapsed* in me," I said, before the words began to tumble out.

"I came back here to pack and realized that with all the in and out of the house, I either misplaced my special family jewelry *or* someone took it during the repairs while we were gone. And if I have to call my crazy landlord, it's going to be a whole thing, and I feel too scatterbrained to be sure either way . . . "

I leaned back against the wall, thinking of the necklace that would be the most devastating to lose: a tiny diamond heart on a white gold chain. It was the first piece of jewelry my dad had given my mom when they were still teenagers, and she had passed it down to me last year. The thought that it might be gone forever was horrifying. How would I ever tell my mom I'd lost something so precious?

I stood again with a lump in my throat that I painfully spoke over:

". . . And I don't even have time to sort it all out, because first of all, I'm not even *supposed* to be in here. And now I have to go catch this flight. I feel like I can't handle packing another bag. I don't even know if I can handle getting on the plane."

Now the tears were streaming. This was the fourth unexpected plane ride in the last six weeks—the fourth time I'd started to exhale, ready to curl up in my room after another intense trip, and then an alarm sounded: *Time to go! Hurry!*

I felt dragged around and burned out from a year of cross-country travel and caregiving for my family back in New York, while trying to keep up with my business and life in California.

Every time I returned in a late-night cab to my place in Venice, it felt like another brick in the foundation of my own life was missing. And lately I couldn't even *remember* what those original bricks looked like in the first place.

I was scrambling to take accountability for everything: money, scheduling, staying organized, getting back to family and friends, and returning to my health routines. I was determined to fix it all, but I couldn't see where to start. I pushed through the sensations, pretending I felt better than I did. And sometimes, I really *did* feel good.

Now even the foundation of my home was compromised. The magic of the beach house was eroding as if it were in the ocean itself, rather than just down the street. But Morgan just smiled.

"Not only can we do a session to release the fear of getting on the plane, but I can pack that suitcase in ten minutes. You need to be able to do that when you're on tour."

Before my friend had become a skilled hypnotherapist, she was a stylist for top musicians, dressing them for their live tours. Even in my panic, I laughed at the synchronicity of it all.

Soon Morgan's hypnotic, even-toned voice was guiding me to the source of the fear. I told her that I was visualizing an airplane ride.

"What's happening on the plane?" she asked.

I saw myself back on the flight to New York six weeks earlier, traveling with my brother Gabe and our uncle Marty. We'd just found out that our beloved 97-year-old grandmother, Bubbie, had been hospitalized. I had just returned home from a long visit on Long Island with her, and Gabe had arrived in L.A. that weekend to spend New Year's at my place. But after a phone call from Mom, we had headed straight to the airport. She had called to tell us that it wasn't likely Bubbie would be leaving the hospital this time, and it was time to come back.

Gabe and I had sat together on the flight, watching a shoddy psychological thriller while sharing a single pair of headphones. The right bud was in his ear, the left in mine. It seemed like the perfect solution—my audio screen wasn't working, and after his recent surgery to remove a tumor from his inner ear canal, Gabe no longer had hearing on the left side anyway.

At the climactic-yet-obvious moment when the bad guy was revealed, I felt a thud and the weight of something on my foot. I looked down to find a man collapsed in the aisle, unconscious.

"Do we have a doctor on board? Can someone help us?" a flight attendant called over the intercom.

Three passengers jumped up, surrounding him, poking and prodding for several minutes. The man didn't move.

"He could be . . . I don't know . . ." one of the doctors muttered.

They knelt as if to begin CPR.

"I think he might be dead," I whispered to Gabe.

But suddenly, the man gasped and opened his eyes, head lolling as he sucked in air.

I came back to my body, the same knot of fear in my stomach that had surfaced on the plane now pulsing again. I heard Morgan's voice gently asking what I was afraid of.

"I'm afraid of someone else dying," I said in a small voice. "I'm afraid of flying into more death."

After a few more minutes, the vision released. Morgan guided me out of the hypnotic state. My body began to stabilize. With relief, I sat back down on the floor, my shoulders dropping. I hadn't realized how the memory of that harrowing moment had remained, right before the final weeks with my grandmother.

"We hold it all in the unconscious," Morgan said.

She had moved on to my suitcase, delicately placing each item inside, folding them so precisely it seemed like they took up no space at all.

"Packing mastery!" I exclaimed.

Morgan laughed. "You have no idea how many silk scarves I've had to fit into a tiny bag."

I sat and watched her. It was faster to let her finish packing than to do it myself. Still, it felt vulnerable to receive this much help, even from a friend. I was used to being the one swooping in with support. But there was a clear divinity in having the perfect person beside me in that moment, and I let myself take it in.

I hugged my friend goodbye, then locked up the house, this time walking right out the front door just as my Uber to LAX pulled up.

I would have to figure out everything else when I got back.

FEBRUARY, 2019: LOS ANGELES, CA

THE WAKE-UP CALL

As the driver took me along the now-familiar route on the 405 toward the airport, I exhaled and fidgeted with my seatbelt, thinking back to the panic attack that had just flooded my system. I could still feel the body memory of it: the cold sweat and involuntary shakes.

I had only experienced a panic attack like that once before. And now, I found myself drifting into the memory of that first time, more than a decade earlier.

It had been a warm June evening. I was twenty-three, in New York City, and at a bar—though the only thing I drank that night was water. I was supposed to be having a fun night out with friends, but I couldn't relax.

My body was tight and drawn; the thinnest I'd ever been after a year of working two jobs, attending two schools, and immersing myself in a nutrition and exercise routine. **Every** moment had become about **output**.

During the 2006–07 school year, I'd commuted monthly to a Manhattan-based health coaching certification while also finishing my last two semesters at Northeastern University in

Boston. The night of the panic attack, I was in New York for the culmination weekend of the coaching program.

When I had graduated from college a week earlier, it was supposed to be a massive celebration for our family. Finishing school while my dad was dying of cancer had been a goal he and my mother clung to. He had passed away at the beginning of my third year.

I could barely feel it, maybe for a few reasons. First of all, I was fixated on the fact that the dramatic, on-again-off-again thing with a local guy had ended for good. It felt consuming at the time, even with no real foundation. The grief of losing my father had folded itself into the ending, and together they blurred into one tide of heartbreak.

More importantly, this was the year I had committed to a new path in healing and spirituality, one I was walking alongside my brother. That pursuit had fully catalyzed after Dad's loss, too.

While I had steadily worked toward my dream career in music journalism since junior high, I no longer knew where it fit into my future. Dad, a lifelong musician and songwriter, had been the champion of that vision. Music was *our* bond. Without him, what did it mean?

How could I possibly return to the life I wanted before all of this?

What I knew for sure was that I didn't want to be like my journalism professor, a woman I had once deeply admired. That had changed the day after the 2004 presidential election, when she walked grimly into class, head down, devastated, like any good New England liberal of the time.

It also happened to be my first week back in school after Dad died. The intensity of his passing and the memorial service that followed had left me raw and reeling. I probably wasn't ready to be there, but I wanted to try, especially during such a relevant political moment for journalism students in Boston. That day, my professor walked up to my desk and handed me my graded paper.

"Alee, you'd better get your writing back on track," she choked out tearfully.

According to her, John Kerry losing to George Bush Jr. was the real tragedy here, and we needed all journalistic hands on deck—if I was still serious about my major.

My face burned. I was stunned. Another student raised her hand to speak up on my behalf, mentioning my recent loss, but somehow that made it worse. My professor didn't budge from her opinion. As journalists, she insisted, our personal lives must never override the news. No one else said anything. We moved on.

That moment became a turning point. I knew then I didn't want to learn from people who treated major life experiences as inconveniences, or who prioritized the "bigger story" over the human beings right in front of them.

I also knew my father had found healing, even if he hadn't survived. I had witnessed profound strength and bravery from him, and from the inner circle around him, that changed my perception of reality. I would finish my journalism degree. But now I also wanted to be in rooms where I could make meaning of what I'd seen in hospitals, to understand life and death in a way that honored what I'd witnessed.

I had always been intuitive, empathetic, and often over-whelmed by it. A sensitivity that felt like both a gift and a curse, depending on the environment. I had never imagined it could be a *career* path. That shifted during this time, when new schools of thought and spiritual teachers entered my life—many of them through Gabe, who was undergoing his own awakening.

Three years before Dad's battle with throat cancer, my brother had faced his own shocking diagnosis: Hodgkin's disease, a cancer of the lymph. Gabe survived. Dad didn't.

It had rearranged everything I thought I knew about our lives; about what mattered and why.

"This is our work now," Gabe said when he wrote me a recommendation letter for the coaching program he had recently completed.

It was the first of what would become many trainings in healing, personal development, and business in the years ahead.

Soon, I began to find my own local metaphysical mentors, and I started the health coaching program where Gabe and I earned the nickname "the Wonder-Siblings."

Suddenly, it felt as though there had never *been* another path but this one. Internally, I had changed majors. By the time I completed my university degree, I had also finished my first coaching certification— and was already working with clients.

It was exhilarating to create these new healing relationships; to witness the positive changes and hopefulness returning in real time. Something meaningful was emerging from our family's pain. For the first time, I was putting this part of myself to real use, beyond being the friend everyone liked venting to.

The passionate excitement I once felt about journalism was now out of reach, replaced by experiencing my sensitives as an actual gift. So I made a new commitment: I would do everything I could to become a practitioner who could thrive in this field, alongside my big brother, the person I loved and admired most of all.

Everything else, even the parts of life that had once brought me so much joy, seemed small in comparison to what I'd witnessed, and what it had awakened in me.

All I wanted was to learn, to grow, to get better.

Always better.

To do it right. To be enough.

To make up for everything that had been lost.

That became the new game.

It was my way of making sense of Gabe's battle and Dad's death. And at twenty-three, this laser focus made me feel secure. If we just learned enough, healed enough, stayed vigilant enough, maybe we could protect ourselves and protect everyone else, too.

And so back in that moment in 2007—the night before I officially received my coaching certification—the weight of my worries disconnected me from my friends and the festive atmosphere. My brain was overcrowded with those pressurized thoughts about what I should be, could be, needed to be doing. And then I had one more question:

Wait, did I remember to ask my roommates to water the plants while I'm gone?

Boom. It was like a final, wobbling Jenga piece; more precarious than anyone could see. That one small thought, delicately sliding loose, brought the whole tower crashing down. I collapsed, trembling, under that same cold sweat.

I could still remember the confused looks on my friends' faces as they looked down at me. I had tried to speak, but nothing came out before I was carried out of the bar by a security guard who assumed I'd been over-served.

Later that night, at a friend's apartment, I called my brother, still in shock.

"This is a big moment for you," he'd said in his signature relaxed tone. "You probably just need to *chill* after so much work. Your body gave you a wake-up call. What's it waking you up to?"

I no longer remember how I answered him, though I do remember the next day ended up being lovely. I was able to slow down and celebrate.

Even so, the slower pace didn't last. There had been fun along the way, but all these years later I was only beginning to understand the weight of the unnecessary pressure I had put on myself.

I loved the work of personal growth. I loved the healing field and the fascinating and magical experiences inside of it. But these days, it felt like I had flown too close to the sun—and been burned more than a few times.

As I sat in the car on the way to the airport, fresh from scaling the side of my own apartment building, the stakes felt so much higher than that night in the bar.

I was now a grown woman, officially five years away from *forty*, with choices to answer for. The decision to hold off on some of the more time-sensitive, traditional life milestones in order to focus on this path was one I had never doubted. But lately, it was starting to feel like something I needed to examine more closely.

I had always assumed there would be time for *everything*. But now, the window felt smaller than ever. Because it was. I could see where I might have afforded myself more spaciousness when I was younger. But now? I didn't feel like I had the time or space to fall apart. I wasn't in my early twenties anymore, with my entire life ahead of me.

And yet just like that long-ago night before graduation, my body was giving me a wake-up call, loud and clear.

It wasn't just the panic attack, though that alone would have been message enough. It had been months of inner struggle. What had began as a whisper was now a shout.

I had felt so strong and fit from my lifestyle, plus yoga and martial arts. But my now muscles ached and there was a new heavy fatigue. My sharp mind was slipping into fog. Lately, it had felt like it took everything in me to simply manage the day-to-day tasks of life. The relationships in L.A. that had once made me feel so deeply connected were loosening with the distance. It had become hard to stay in touch in between the trips.

It was scary to admit that after a series of the most exciting and prosperous years in my business, I was struggling to keep up with the pace I had once so eagerly set. My clients were pleased and the work was still fulfilling. But inside, I felt too worn out to keep growing the way I used to.

As the cab driver pulled up to departures and I grabbed my luggage, I heard my brother's words again:

Your body just gave you a wake-up call. What is it waking you up to?

I hoped this trip—and some time with Gabe—would tell me.

FEBRUARY, 2019: MIAMI BEACH, FL

THE MANATEES

*B*y the next morning, I was driving across a bridge surrounded by shimmering waters, candy-colored buildings, and lush palms that were nostalgic of my childhood. Our grandparents, aunt, and cousin had moved from New York to Miami Beach in the late 1980s, so growing up, my family had spent many school breaks here.

And now Gabe was the newest full-time resident, ready for a fresh start after a wild year that culminated in the freedom to come down and give it a shot. I rode past the iconic pastel pink *WELCOME TO MIAMI BEACH* sign, and soon I was just a few minutes away from his new place.

I got out of the cab and the familiar blanket of humidity enveloped me as I walked up to the bright white building and entered what looked like the waiting room of a luxury spa. The smell of eucalyptus wafted through the air, and Zen stone sculptures were displayed beside expensive-looking wicker furniture and long glass tables. The patio doors opened out onto a massive infinity pool with the sparkling Miami Bay as its backdrop.

I texted Gabe:

I'm here!

As I took in the scene, I recalled my brother's last apartment, a simple walk-up in Brooklyn that he had shared with his fiancee at the time. And then, even more recently, my own childhood bedroom, where he stayed while recovering from surgery. It was a room more aptly sized for a baby than a grown man.

This upgraded home base was truly the start of something new for him after so much intensity.

I walked up to the front desk and was greeted by a young woman with braids sculpted into an elegant updo. She wore a silky purple blouse and a dazzling smile. As I looked around, I realized that *everything* in Gabe's apartment complex felt special and beautiful, including the staff.

Although for the last few days Gabe had been staying in a furnished apartment the building kept for guests, today he would begin a lease of his own.

"Hi, I'm here to meet Gabe Hoffman? I'm his sister, Alee. He just moved into his apartment this morning."

She took down my name and then told me in a friendly tone to have a seat, as he would have to come down to get me. I rolled my suitcase over to a brown suede couch and sank into the plush cushion. I texted Gabe again:

In your building. AMAZING! So happy for you!

He quickly responded:

Awesome <3. On a call. Down in a few.

A few minutes turned into twenty, and then it was over an hour of sitting on that couch as I watched people stride in and out of the front lobby to Alton Road, or stroll through the lounge to the pool with a towel and magazine folded under their arm.

The novelty of this lovely space was fading, and the reality of my exhaustion started to take hold. I had flown overnight, and I starting to feel an aversion to the loud music, sun-drenched room, and perky people. I texted Gabe again:

Dude what the hell!!

Finally, Gabe came down, breezing into the lobby with his broad shoulders and solid posture, the result of a daily Qigong routine. He was still talking business on his headset, not having missed a beat. He gave me a hug and then grabbed my bag, silently motioning for me to follow him.

I sighed dramatically but got up to walk behind him, knowing my annoyance was already dissipating. I was just too happy to see my brother, to feel the safety and comfort his presence always brought, even when he was distracted. And I was too happy *for* him; to witness him thriving in a new environment after everything he had been through lately.

By now, Gabe was fifteen years into his career in holistic medicine, and always focused on the next new research, routine, or food to stay healthy. And he *was* very healthy, seeming to grow stronger with each year that took him further away from his last cancer treatment at age twenty-one.

But now after all those years of growing in vitality, something had shifted; Gabe hadn't felt like himself. First it was tinnitus in his ears, then a sensitivity to heat and loud noises, which ultimately gave way to anxiety from feeling so off-kilter. We wondered if it was some sort of detox- did the treatments that had once saved his life now linger in his body like a dormant poison?

He went to a doctor and got the diagnosis: acoustic neuroma, a benign tumor in the inner ear canal.

For most people, an acoustic neuroma eventually requires brain surgery to remove it. It also means losing hearing in that ear.

They gave Gabe a year to see if the tumor would stay small and he could avoid surgery.

He explored treatment options and requested information from some of the most renowned medical practitioners and researchers in his network. Then Gabe dropped deeply into a Qigong practice: first as a student and then, extraordinarily quickly, as a new teacher with a growing community. It was inspiring and empowering. But it didn't stop the tumor. And so finally, he had gone back to the doctors to bravely face the next step of surgery. It couldn't be avoided.

Now he no longer had hearing on his left side, which we jokingly referred to as his "good" ear. When someone started to tell him something he didn't feel like listening to—or our mom would nag a bit—he would say:

"Sorry, didn't catch that, can you say it into my good ear?" as he angled the left side of his face toward them.

If I was in the room we would start cackling. Even when he said it to me, I would still laugh.

Despite the jokes, my brother had changed again. I had watched different diagnoses and treatments change him since we were teenagers.

The first big one had been many years ago, after his second turn with Hodgkin's. He came out of the coma and steadily regained his life as a young man, only to watch our dad's own diagnosis and battle begin. Gabe drove Dad to the same radiation appointments that our father had once taken him to.

After losing our father, Gabe became more aggressive and self-protective until he found a way to channel the experience into a life purpose and career. In those years, successfully becoming a functional medicine entrepreneur had transformed him once more: he bloomed with confidence and enthusiasm.

This time, the new diagnosis—although non-cancerous—was still significant and brought up the memories of the relapses both he and Dad had faced. He had been destabilized again, right as the responsibilities in his life had grown.

Gabe's sense of humor was still in there, but the silliness had been replaced with more rigidity and an overall serious presence. He was unyielding about when he went to bed, when he needed to eat, taking all his supplements, doing his practices. He had stopped drinking or smoking pot some years ago, but now he wouldn't even have caffeine.

I missed my more playful, even mischievous, brother.

The old Gabe had been deeply passionate about his work and purpose but still gregariously social. That version of him who would go dancing until late and then grab a slice on the way home, cracking jokes the whole way. The one who was up for spontaneous road trips and live music and hilarious adventures, woven in with business development and deep talks about anything and everything.

These recent health challenges had kept him in a life that was smaller and more sheltered than what was true to his spirit. During his recovery, he and his fiancée came to see that their relationship was not meant to continue, and the engagement came to an end. The wedding plans, and all the effort to weave together two very different families, were called off.

Suddenly, it was all over. Yet in many ways, the hardest part was behind him too: the distressing diagnosis, the frightening surgery. Those chapters were in the past now. The painful decisions had been made, and both could begin to heal.

Recovery was underway, and my brother was back on the road to creating a life rich with adventure once again.

It was just the beginning.

We took the elevator up, Gabe still responding to questions on the phone the whole way. Finally—blessedly—he hung up, as the elevator reached his floor and the doors opened.

We entered the outdoor walkway lined with apartments and patio furniture until we reached his new door: *1122.* Twenty-two was our father's special, lifelong number, and anytime we saw it, we felt his presence. A spiritual nudge.

Gabe opened the door to the clean, open canvas of his new apartment, with all the condo-like trimmings that come in a fancy unit: marble countertops, smooth white walls, and gleaming stainless-steel appliances.

He placed my suitcase by the door, and we turned back around. The view was so fabulous and so unlike where my brother had lived before that we both started to laugh at the luxury and how easily it had come together for him in just a matter of days.

In front of us was an expanse of blue sky dotted with puffy white clouds and the Miami Beach skyline of high-rises. Just below that was turquoise water, a small pier, and a sea of manatees. Their thick, rounded backs surfaced as they somersaulted before diving under again, creating slow, graceful flashes of dark brown and silver.

I ran up to the banister and looked down. "Gabe! How amazing is this?" I called out.

The manatees popped their heads out of the water again, taking loud, heaving breaths that spurted droplets. With their curvaceous bodies, I could sort of see how once upon a time, sailors might have thought these animals were mermaids. Mermaids with asthma, perhaps.

As we looked down, we watched two manatees swim toward each other from opposite sides of the water, nearly embracing like it was an epic reunion.

"He's like, 'Where you been? I haven't seen you in a month!'" Gabe said, using his voice reserved for impersonating animals whenever they looked to be having a human moment.

It was a sunny February morning with a balmy tropical breeze, and I got to be with my best friend as he opened the door to a new chapter in a new city. And now there were *manatees* greeting us. I tabled my own worries and put my focus on Gabe and his successful move.

2019 was going to be his year.

Before heading back inside, the next door neighbor Henry told us this was the first time since he'd moved in that the manatees had ever swum up to the water below the terrace like this.

My brother and I took this as a special sign, as we did with most notable things that happened around us, especially on an auspicious day like move-in. Gabe did a quick web search on his phone for manatee symbolism. He looked up and his deep grayish blue eyes—just like mine—stared back meaningfully.

"This one's for you, Al. Manatees symbolize compassion, slowing down, and acceptance. Deep acceptance of how it all is, right at this moment."

I thought of the situation I had just flown away from, and my throat tightened. I hadn't realized how wonderfully distracted the time together had made me until that moment. Everything I had just flown from came rushing back.

There was so much to work out. My eyes filled with emotion, and I put my hands up to my face. He noticed and asked:

"What's going on? Having a hard time today?"

I felt the warm tears roll down my cheeks and exhaled into a laugh at the relief of being with my big brother and not having to pretend.

"Dude, I'm all over the place. I almost couldn't get on the plane last night because I was having a fucking *panic* attack." I squeezed the white banister in front of me as I talked. "Everything feels off, like I'm going backward in time, losing everything."

Gabe listened intently, his breath deep and steady. He sat down on a chair across from me, giving me space to be in the emotion of the moment. I took one last big inhale to get out my final sentence.

"I keep circling to, 'What is happening here? What am I doing wrong? Where can I change it?'"

My brother paused and then gently responded.

"So right now, you're seeing your life through the lens of *you* being the problem. You're not the problem. You've never been the problem, Al. You're *always* going to be the solution in your own life."

I tried to let the words in like a soothing tonic, to really feel them as true. I could understand that a solution would first need to have a relationship with the problem. But the speed at which I was feeling out of control frightened me.

I was afraid of believing that this moment could be the turn-around and then being disappointed. Or worse, what if I was wasting precious time? I had this ever-deepening sense that time was running out. In some ways, it was a familiar feeling.

My teens and twenties had pulsed with the need to catch up and keep up; to stay on course while my family journeyed through the experience of illness. The years meant for development through self-focus were paired with hospital visits, while trying to keep it together and not have to ask for another extension at school.

Celebration and socializing had always been important in my family, even during hard times. The way our house had been the landing spot for so many legendary events, so too became my dorm rooms and first apartments. I loved that—but it didn't leave much space for grief.

And after a youth spent in close proximity to loss, I'd traversed my twenties immersed in the art and craft of healing and entrepreneurship, often with people twice my age. These things combined would often have me lose sight of how *young* I actually was at the time.

I could now see where I hadn't understood that sometimes, literal life experience, just time itself, was required for the business goals I'd set and the spiritual wisdom I was seeking. That lack of perspective had resulted in a lot of self-induced pressure and a chronic sense that I needed to be further along than I already was.

But the first years of my thirties had blossomed into a wonderful time of feeling like I was exactly where I wanted to be.

Was I losing that already?

As the first week in Miami with my brother unfolded, I took a break from those thoughts and got immersed in the fun of setting up Gabe's awesome new life.

We bought furniture and supplies for his place; couches and beach towels and teal-colored pots and pans. We ordered Indian food and watched old favorites like *Trading Places* and those ridiculous *Fyre Festival* documentaries, the newest additions to our ever-growing collection of inside jokes.

We strolled down Collins Avenue, buying crystals and plants before settling into a laminated wood table at Puerto Sagua, the old-school Cuban restaurant in South Beach that we'd gone to since we were little kids visiting with our grandparents.

I ordered our usual #22 roast chicken special, poured tangy orange mystery dressing on the avocado salad, and felt at home.

As I watched my brother explore his new environment, I could see that more of his joyful personality was returning. The strain had lessened: he was laughing more and even treated himself to an after-lunch coffee.

"Gabe is back," my mom had said to me on the phone that week, when I told her how the visit was going. She continued:

"Thank God. This is what he needed. It's what he needed all along."

One afternoon we went to Whole Foods to stock up his kitchen. We stopped in the candle aisle and Gabe asked me which one I thought he needed. I had felt drawn to a black protection candle. But he ended up choosing the blue one, which symbolized good health.

After it all happened, I thought back to those candles with magical thinking, gripping to any detail that could have prevented what came next.

Could it have stopped anything if he had picked up the black one instead?

MARCH, 2019: MIAMI BEACH, FL

THE UNKNOWN FUTURE

I slid into the smooth cushioned booth. The interior was dark and cool, and there was hip-hop playing as the Friday night rush began. I looked across the table: Gabe was in his favorite aqua button-down and Mom wore a flowing black sundress. They were looking at the menu together and already planning what we should share. The joy in having a great meal to honor the milestones in life was definitely a family pastime.

Mom had gotten to town that morning, and made this dinner plan to celebrate mine and Gabe's recent birthdays. We took a dressed-up family selfie on his terrace as the moon rose over the bay. Then we walked over over to Macchialina, a nearby Italian restaurant and one of the hippest dining spots in Miami. It was going to be an excellent meal.

When Gabe had first told me Mom was on her way, I was apprehensive. Although I had seen my mother frequently in the last few months, I was hoping to look a little different the next time I saw her. Every recent visit with Mom came with more concern and what felt to me like criticism about how I seemed— too tired, too puffy, too much of one thing or another.

Our mother, Gina, is a Jewish New Yorker; a brilliant interior designer with a flair for color and style. She's notorious for her fabulous outfits and accessories and her gift for entertaining, with party themes and decorations that nobody else could replicate. Our birthdays, back-to-school celebrations, holidays, and family parties were known for her attention to every little detail. Even our dad's memorial—and the ensuing "Chuck-Fests" of live music gatherings with his former band—were extraordinarily memorable and fun events.

But given her history and sharp eye, I would also regularly hear:

"Alee, I've been through too much. You can't make me worry any more than I have to. And I will *always* worry."

And yet so far this short visit with her had been pleasant; without any of the now-regular commentary about how I was doing. I suspected Gabe had told her to tone it down, at least for now.

For our birthday meal, we decided to do the special tasting menu Macchialina was known for: finely shaved prosciutto, homemade pastas, savory polenta with fresh marinara, and a refreshingly icy espresso granita on top of creamy tiramisu, paired with some amazing red wine.

Many years ago, back home on Long Island, I had once been a server at an Italian restaurant alongside Jackie, now the sommelier and co-owner of Macchialina with her brothers, so we received especially delightful attention and service.

When we got back to Gabe's, I fell asleep quickly—full from the decadent dinner and soothed by the sound of Gabe and Mom chatting. It reminded me of when I was a child, listening to the sound of my dad's band practicing in our living room, which was right below my bedroom. I was always lulled by the soft vibration of guitars and quiet laughter. Or the sound of my mother closing up the kitchen before heading to bed, the final click and whoosh as she pressed the dishwasher door into place and turned it on.

The next day I sat in the ocean with my eyes closed, the cool water up to my chest and warm sunshine on the top of my head. Mom and Gabe sat in a yellow-striped cabana further back in the sand. After this final afternoon together at the beach, I would be flying back to Los Angeles. The remediation for the mold issue in my building was officially complete, and apparently, all was clear to move back in.

Last night before we headed to our birthday dinner, Gabe had suggested that I live with him for a while. I wanted to say yes, but I also knew I needed to say no—at least for now.

Sure, I could stay here for a while; deflate the blow-up mattress each morning, tuck it back into the corner of his living room, and pretend the complications across the country didn't exist. But that would be an escape. As it was, I had already spent months away with all our family stuff going on. It was time to go back to L.A. and figure it out.

I knew if I stayed with Gabe, I would feel relief and purpose from being around him. I could simply follow along with his jam-packed schedule: he was so busy at the moment with two businesses and teaching. But I needed to confront what was happening in my *own* life.

Maybe when the cab pulled up late at night this time, I would feel like I had located those missing pieces. Even if it just meant preparing to move out.

As I sat with my thoughts in the ocean, I steadied myself with the decision not to hide inside my brother's life or energy. I had first seen this pattern years earlier, after returning home from college. As close as we were, living in the same place left me too content to orbit his ideas and follow his lead. I soon realized I wasn't fully honoring my own direction—and although similar to Gabe's, it was never meant to be the same.

A year later, that realization pushed me into motion. I left New York for Chicago, determined to step out of the little sister role in the projects we were both working on. Ever the big brother, Gabe still supported me in that leap by driving with me all the way out there on what became one of our favorite road trip memories, before taking the car back to New York once I was settled. I had needed a life that was distinctly mine, even though part of me wanted to stay close. From then on, Gabe and I never lived in the same city again, but our connection never wavered. We always knew the other was just a phone call or visit away.

When I moved to Chicago, it marked the start of an adventurous post-college life. I quickly fell in love with the city: the people, the rhythm, the way of life. It was also where I first encountered an energetic tool that would soon become the foundation of my spiritual practice: the Akashic Records, a form of metaphysical connection and energy work.

Over time, the Records became my most powerful path for healing and discovery, much the way others might find resonance with Tarot or plant medicine. I often describe them as the Universe's spiritual supercomputer: like a vast, non-physical library containing the stories and energies of *everything* — our lives, relationships, creative projects, even places and events. They all carry a kind of energetic file that can be opened and explored.

I enter the Records by dropping into a meditative state and reciting a special prayer that acts like a key. Once inside, the field reveals itself through energy I translate into words, guidance, healings, writing, and art.

My first encounter, guided by another practitioner, felt like coming home. It was as if I had always known this space, and now remembered how to access it. From there, my channeling and creative abilities began to expand and unfold in ways I could never have imagined. The Records didn't deliver a script to act out, but became a steady ally and teacher, with loving guidance for myself and my clients.

Learning to translate energy was like learning a new language.

After years of daily practice and thousands of sessions, I became quite fluent. Through this work I've had the honor of supporting clients around the world and teaching others to connect with the Records themselves. What began as a practice of healing became a source of meaningful work, community, and countless profound experiences.

And yet, even with all this energetic support, I was still a person in a rough spot. Nothing supernatural cancels out the truth—the human experience brings challenges we cannot always immediately meet.

I knew Gabe and Mom had been having conversations about her concern for me while we were together those days. I clearly was not myself, although I kept insisting to them that I just needed some time, after all the upheaval of this past year, to reprioritize and refocus on my *own* life.

Inside, I was anxious and ashamed, more so than I wanted anyone to know. So much of what I had worked for so long toward, in both my personal and professional life, had actualized. And now, it felt like it was slowly fading away. I didn't know if it could come back, even with my gifts.

Perhaps this was all I was supposed to have, I thought.

At the moment, it all still looked "good" to most people. But deep down, I felt something was off.

When had that happened?

I could have sworn I had done it all "right."

Before leaving the water, I decided it was time to go into the Akasha and receive a message to bring back home with me. I recited my prayer and felt the energetic access open to the Record of my life as the waves gently lapped around me. A rush of warmth washed over my body as my head softened, the way it always did when the Records were opened.

The peace of this energy field was always here, no matter what else was happening. I asked for any guidance about my return to L.A. that could help with my next steps.

I heard the response back. It was gentle but definitive:

You are about to be tested beyond anything you have ever experienced. However, you will be provided for the entire time, as you always have been, and as you always will be.

I contracted my body and scrunched up my nose as if to reject the answer. I silently asked the field:

How much more could I be tested? It's felt so hard already. How do I prevent what's coming next?

Sometimes the Akashic Records respond through the physical environment rather than a psychic message. At that moment, I heard water sputter with a heavy gasp of breath, and my eyes blinked open.

Six feet in front of me, right there in South Beach—packed with Spring Breakers, loud music, and helicopter advertisements— a manatee squinted at me head-on.

It caught my gaze, then slowly went back under, swimming away toward a calmer space on the horizon.

This was my answer and a reminder from the first day Gabe moved in: There was nothing to prevent or change, just an unknown future to accept.

Before I got into the cab to the airport, Gabe gave me his signature goodbye—a warm hug that transitioned into a high five—as he said:

"Hey, I trust you, like, *implicitly*. I'm never really worried about you. Because whatever happens, I know you'll figure it out. You always do."

There had been a period of time when it felt like I *had* figured it all out. But after this year, as I heard Gabe's certainty, I wasn't so certain myself.

I wondered with some trepidation what was waiting in L.A., after that Akashic message I received on the beach.

But as I turned around and got into the car, I decided it was time to lean into my brother's unending belief in me with the same confidence I always carried for him.

APRIL, 2019: LOS ANGELES, CA

THE DOCTOR'S OFFICE

One month later, I found myself sitting in a doctor's office waiting room in Marina del Rey. Despite trying to psych myself up for my return to L.A., the fatigue, inflammation, and down feelings had worsened since my trip to Gabe's.

My housemates and I were back in the building with a mix of caution and hope that the situation had been properly resolved. Our landlord assured us that everything was fine—remediation and painting crews had worked on our apartments for a month. According to her, the toxic mold was gone, and we should no longer be experiencing any symptoms.

What I would discover later on was that this wasn't actually true. Being exposed to the mold for two years had already impacted my health greatly, and that wouldn't change just because they had finally discovered and remediated it. But at the time, I didn't know the real implications of the situation. I wanted to believe the worst was over.

The first week in April, I woke up with a throat so swollen I could barely swallow. At this point, my roommate Kimiko was worried. She calmly yet firmly guided me outside to her Jeep and drove me to the closest UCLA Health center with an available appointment.

Outside, the sun glinted off the water and onto a series of boats with names like *Feelin' Nauti* and *The Codfather.* Inside, I sat crying with my assigned doctor—a sturdy-looking woman in her sixties with a glamorous mane of blonde hair and a thick Swedish accent. Dr. Hansen looked over her horn-rimmed glasses at me with concern.

She had just asked me about the health history of my immediate family members, a question that usually choked me up in a doctor's office anyway, but now sent me into convulsing sobs that shocked me with their ferocity.

My blood tests showed an abnormally high white blood cell count, a potential marker for cancer. Dr. Hansen ordered X-rays to scan for tumors, then frowned at my swollen throat. Even before the exam began, the scale in the hallway had delivered its own shock: 201 pounds. At five-foot-three, I had gained around forty pounds this year.

At first glance, I was shocked into silence. It seemed that no matter how healthy I had tried to be, the weight I always feared gaining had finally caught up to me.

I could freely admit to myself that even the white blood cell count didn't rattle me in quite the same way. I didn't know what was happening to me, but I'd been around cancer for much of my life. I knew instinctively this wasn't that.

But being overweight had felt like something I had been constantly staving off with exercise and diet since childhood. My physicality had always been a lightning rod for the energy and messages it carried in ways that held both gifts and challenges. Whatever I was going through, be it joyous or hard, had always seemed to be immediately perceptible just by looking at me. And whatever this new energy was, my body knew it was heavy—in every sense of the word.

My mind flashed to the scene in the movie *Something About*

Mary, when Matt Dillon's character discourages Ben Stiller from pursuing Mary, the girl they both love. Dillon falsely describes her current weight, hoping to throw Stiller off by pretending she had gained a lot as an adult.

"Oh, she's about a deuce, deuce and a half."

I remembered my brother and his friends laughing hysterically at this line when we were kids. It was more about Dillon's delivery, and the fact that Mary was actually the lithe and leggy Cameron Diaz. Still, something in my pre-teen brain registered a message that stuck:

Do not become any chubbier or you will be the punchline.

Next, my mind flashed to a line in an Oprah Winfrey weight-loss book from the 90s that sat on the coffee table at my aunt's house. On hot summer afternoons I'd sit on the couch on the back porch reading and re-reading it when there was nothing else to do. In the opening chapter, Oprah wrote that she knew she'd hit rock bottom when Mike Tyson was crowned the Heavyweight Boxing Champion of the World at 218 pounds. In that moment, she realized she was heavier than *The* Heavyweight, and could live that way no more.

It turned out that line had been living in me like a time-released pill, waiting to cascade forward the moment I, too, neared Mike Tyson's 1986 boxing weight.

Then, Dr. Hansen spoke.

"Right now, I don't know what's wrong with you, physically speaking. I can't explain *why* you are having these symptoms or the high white cell count, not yet. But what I *can* tell you is that you're definitely having a depressive episode."

She paused and looked at me gently.

"It's understandable. You've had a hard year; you lost your grandmother, you had a scary experience with your brother's surgery, you've had all this travel and change. It's made you tired and sad. I'm going to write you a referral to the psychology department. And I'm also going to write you a prescription for an antidepressant. I hope you'll fill it."

The appointment ended, and I opened the clinic door and walked out into the breezy warmth, clutching the folder of unsettling information as I decided to walk home. It was still a beautiful day. The sun was high in the sky, which meant it was already late afternoon in New York City. Gabe's doctor's appointment would be finished, too.

Thirty minutes later, on the phone with him, my stress was beginning to dissipate. Gabe had gotten great news from his doctors: his surgical recovery was right on track, and the heart valve issue that had been flagged during pre-op was mild enough to monitor over time.

"Hey, proud of you," I said as I stood with my eyes closed in the sunshine. "I know what it took for you to go back to a traditional doctor."

It meant being back in the rooms where it all started. Where he had once felt so powerless.

"Yeah," he replied softly. "It did bring me back to the second time around, from what I remember of it. I've blocked a lot out, but I'm pretty sure I fell out of my chair when they told me."

Gabe's second bout with Hodgkin's was in some ways more shocking than the first. After spending the majority of his senior year in high school doing chemo and radiation, Gabe had been told he had a "basically zero" chance of ever relapsing. He went off to college with his best friends, James and Sean, as his dormmates. The rest of us filed it away as the surreal year where Gabe got sick, but we rallied together and he triumphed. He was better, and nothing else needed to change.

But then came his regular follow-up, right before heading back to school for sophomore year. That appointment changed everything. The cancer was back, and it was aggressive. That day marked the beginning of the harsher treatments. The coma. Then, in the aftermath, we found out about Dad's throat cancer diagnosis.

That fateful appointment had revealed the truth: *nothing* about this time could simply be filed away. It was an initiation into a new life path, for all of us.

"I remember something like that with Dad, too," I said, my chest tightening with my own memory of being hit with frightening news right after hope had been offered.

My mind wandered back to my senior year of high school. It was January 2002, a school night in the coldest part of winter. I sat by my dad as he lay in bed at Huntington Hospital, and *Law & Order: SVU* flickered on the tiny TV above our heads. Dad had never been into crime shows, but he knew it was my favorite one.

A few minutes later, his doctor arrived to check his vitals.

I was not usually in the room alone with the doctor, and for some reason that night I found my confidence to follow him out and ask a question nobody else seemed to want to answer.

"Excuse me," I said in my most mature voice. "Is my father going to be okay?"

The doctor looked at me with a brief smile before replying in a clipped tone:

"Oh sure. He's getting the treatment he needs."

He kept walking to his next appointment, and I smiled back, relieved, turning to head back to Dad's room.

But then the doctor said one more thing:

"Of course, if he gets this again, he will die."

I remembered how easily he had said it, so flat and definitive. Never breaking stride, never looking up from his folder. Next was the shock and fear that rocked my body. And then, in the next moment, the decision to put his words away, to hide them somewhere deep inside myself.

After one year of remission, my dad's cancer returned just before I started my second year of college. At the time, it seemed like my parents were very hopeful about his prognosis. But when they told me, I instantly thought about what the doctor had said to me that cold winter night. I figured if my parents were this optimistic, maybe the doctor hadn't told *them*. So, I kept the self-created vow of silence.

It was almost funny to me now, the way I had believed that me —and *only* me—the youngest member of the family, had been given the bad news about Dad. My teenage self decided it was my job to keep my parents in blissful ignorance of his predicted demise.

What I've observed over the years in other families going through long-term illness, is that everyone eventually takes on secret missions; roles they are *sure* they've been asked to play, even when no one else even knows they're doing it. We think we're taking it on to protect others from pain, but really, it protects us too.

This sense of life-or-death responsibility began with Gabe's first diagnosis the summer before I started high school. From there, it followed me into every relationship: friends, lovers, bosses, teachers, clients. The sense of obligation was dense and unyielding and, I now suspected, had not always been actually requested.

In the last year of my father's life, he wrote and recorded an album of songs about his healing journey, his mortality, and his love for everyone. The song for Mom was one of my favorites. It was called *Love Survives* and told the story of his falling in love with her in their youth, and how he imagined he would stay connected to her after his death. The chorus was:

> *So tell me why, why, why*
> *They try and make us cry*
> *Shake their heads and sigh*
> *Don't even say goodbye*
> *Don't wanna hear that jive*
> *I've never felt so alive*

*That's why my heart replies—**Love survives***

After Dad died, I would listen to the song and recognize that he obviously *had* experienced the same kind of conversations with the doctors. Years later, Mom told me that regardless of what the doctors said, they really did believe Dad had a chance to beat the odds; that they weren't playing pretend for my benefit.

Still, I had never told anyone what the doctor had said to me.

Back in the current moment, I wondered if that was how Gabe had held the experience of that second diagnosis inside: his own vow of silence until now. He never told me how it felt to hear the news, and somehow, even with all we had shared, I'd never asked.

But now, he could say it. In my heart I felt the warmth of relief.

"Well, you confronted wherever that memory has been living inside you," I said, "And now you know for sure it's okay. So, what's the next step?"

I was getting closer to my house in Venice, the view shifting from glossy, commercial Marina del Rey into my neighborhood with its brick walls splashed with colorful street art and graffiti. A group of skateboarders rolled past me on their way to the ocean-side bowl.

"The doctor says whatever I've been feeling in my chest is just *anxiety* from everything that's been happening," Gabe answered, his voice full of lightness. "He said I can start to push beyond it on a treadmill. So that's the next step. When I get back to Miami, I'm gonna get back in the gym."

I looked at the sun coming through the palm trees as I slowly walked down the street, soaking in the gratitude that my brother's years of worry were finally being put down.

The gravity of that thought hit me. I contemplated that maybe he had secretly been living in fear of raising his heart rate while still trying to live the full life of a healthy man in his thirties: hiking, traveling, sex, having a fun night out. He had focused on staying calm and steady for so long. But now Gabe could finally begin to loosen the grip of control and go beyond his own self-created limit — starting with the treadmill.

"So," he chuckled, "that was *my* doctor's appointment. What about yours?"

I paused and took a breath before answering. "Well, I definitely have issues. But the doctor doesn't know what's wrong with me, besides telling me I'm depressed." I took a moment to admire a bird of paradise blooming in front of an office building before adding, "Then again, I pretty much always cry in the doctor's office. Have you ever thought about what it's like to share *our* family's history with a doctor?"

I impersonated the way Dr. Hansen had reacted to the family medical history questionnaire earlier that day:

"And what about your *mawder*? Ooh, okay. And how about your *fawdher*? Oh wow, that's too bad. And your *brudher*? Oh goodness, oh no. Uncles? Grandparents? *Yikes.*"

Pretty soon we were laughing, despite it all. And within the laughter, I felt something shift: a powerful merging happening between us. An understanding of each other's experiences that went beyond having *witnessed* them to now having *lived* them, too.

I pointed it out to Gabe:

"I feel like I understand a bit more how it must have felt for you. Having to go to scary meetings with doctors, where you don't know what you'll hear."

Gabe replied, as if in deep thought, "I feel that. And now I can go to these appointments and hear it's all good. Soon you will, too."

I hoped he was right.

APRIL, 2019: LOS ANGELES, CA

THE FULL MOON RITUAL

I sat cross-legged on the floor in front of my bedroom altar. A pale stripe of moonlight and the sound of crashing waves drifted softly through my open window.

In front of me were several stones: an ink-black obsidian for protection, a large pink rose quartz for love, and a double-sided smoky quartz, pale blue on both points, to activate my intentions. A large rocky piece of purple amethyst with a small divot holding a burning candle was the only light in the room. It cast dancing shadows on the wall.

The crystals encircled black-and-white photos of my grandmothers, my dad's album cover, fresh white roses in a slim glass vase, a small piece of palo santo, and my notebook and pen. These were all typical pieces on my altar when I was preparing to drop into ceremony. But next to them sat something I had never brought into this space before: a small plastic orange bottle with a child-safety cap.

The label listed two names: one for the oval-shaped white pills inside—Lexapro. The other for the person they were prescribed to — me.

I had picked up the bottle that afternoon from a local CVS. The pharmacy was in the back, and I walked a merry rainbow-hued gauntlet of Peeps alongside solemn-faced chocolate bunnies, both waiting for their last chance to be dropped into Easter baskets.

Since Gabe and I had gone to our simultaneous doctor appointments ten days earlier, I'd tried to stay calm and focus on the blessings. He was going to be fine and my scans had come back negative for any markers of cancer. I made plans with friends and went on a couple dates with a guy I had paused things with when I'd been out of town so often. I took my daily beach walks with a prayer to feel better.

Last weekend, I'd traveled to Portland to host a group Akashic Records experience and attend my friend's dance performance. I came home in time for the going-away party of my downstairs neighbors. We made a bonfire and laughed as we drank white wine from plastic cups and watched the sky turn brilliant colors at sunset.

I tried to stay focused on the fact that even though it would *always* be a sad year, having lost Bubbie at the start of it, there was still goodness. And yet, in between these lovely moments, large waves of what felt like the *deepest* grief and yearning would crash over me. It tightened my chest and brought fresh tears to my eyes. While in Portland, I sat on cold soil under a dark green fir and cried. When I returned to Venice, I rested my back against a sandy palm tree and wept.

"It actually feels like I'm grieving *Gabe*," I told a friend when the tears first came. "Maybe because now that we know he's really going to be okay, I can finally let myself feel all the worry I've been holding inside and let it all go?"

That was my best understanding of the sorrow living inside my chest. I knew it had been there for a long time, and perhaps it finally had permission to be seen.

There had been a loyalty to my brother and to the rest of my family for many years now; a vow to not be totally devastated. To be inspired more than impacted by the years of sickness and the loss of Dad. To focus on what it had *given* me in purpose and wisdom, rather than what had been taken in my youth.

And while Dad was gone, we still had Gabe. We all quietly wondered if somehow my father had taken on the diagnosis for his son.

"If I could take this from him, I would," Dad had said, in some of the darkest hours in the ICU.

Over the past week, Gabe had been texting me—in between pictures of manatees and funny memes—that he'd spoken to colleagues who believed the mold in my apartment could be far more severe than I realized. Their opinion: even after the remediation, I should be moving out ASAP.

I heard that. I wanted to move. But it all felt so hard. *Everything* did.

I wouldn't learn until later that fatigue and brain fog are hallmarks of mold illness. All I knew at the time was that I had hit a new wall of sadness, and my mind was discovering dark and unfamiliar territory.

Until then, I had always known how to find meaning in the hard things, no matter the commitment required. Life had delivered a lot of intensity and challenge, but I had never stopped wanting to be part of it. To *do* and share something from what I'd experienced.

Still, I could empathize with people walking this edge. In our early twenties, a beloved life-long friend and neighbor of ours had ended his life after years of trying to hold on. Gabe and I loved him dearly; his gentle, artist's soul, and deep reverence for the healing wisdom of nature had shaped and inspired us both. His presence was a part of many favorite childhood memories. And yet, as the years went on, all he knew and practiced could not outweigh the inner battle he carried. His death, just a year after

Dad's, was another big catalyst in our understanding of the non-physical and infinite realm.

I had also sat in this space with clients who struggled in this same way or found themselves encountering it as they touched painful realizations in their history. Sometimes I would make the call to refer them to mental health professionals to anchor more support.

But now, something in *me* was shifting. The part of me that always wanted to participate was starting to dim. When I zoomed out as an observer, it was humbling. It gave me a deeper understanding of what I'd witnessed in others. But when I zoomed back in—as the one living it—it was frightening.

At the end of the second week in April, I dialed Gabe's number and hoped he would answer.

"I don't want to freak you out," I said through tears, "but I'm almost starting to feel like I don't really want to, like, *live* anymore. Or like I don't have the energy to figure out what's wrong. It's all just feeling wrong. Like something bad is happening."

As a student of the human experience, I could still see I didn't really want to end my life as much as I wanted to end the exhaustion. I wanted to stop carrying the confusion about what to do next, to stop feeling like I was losing the best parts of myself.

I wanted a do-over.

The despair was starting to reframe even joyful times as nothing more than crumbs scattered along a relentlessly rocky path.

As always, Gabe responded with calm compassion.

"Hey, you're gonna be alright. But it's time to get more help."

We talked about a new plan that included therapy and the medication my doctor had suggested a couple of weeks earlier. It was humbling, but I was ready to loop in a type of support that hadn't been a part of my life until now. Anything was better than this.

After our call, I walked out the back porch, down the sandy

block with the ocean crashing ahead of me, until I reached the end of my street. The big sign right before me read *DEAD END*.

I took off my shoes and padded into the sand, sitting heavily on the ground as I watched the sun drop into the ocean. I wanted to stop thinking this way. I wanted to stop scaring myself and my brother.

I would follow through on my promise to him and go get the antidepressants.

The following day I texted Gabe in front of a CVS, straddling my pink beach cruiser, one foot still on the curb:

> Got the Lexapro.

He responded with a picture of his hand holding a little stuffed sloth with a perfectly round head and big sparkling eyes—both strikingly like Gabe himself. The tiny red tag on its sleeve said his name was "Dangles," and that he was born on 2/22—the lucky numbers.

I had bought the stuffed animal for Gabe at a gas station the previous winter when we were driving home from holiday shopping and he'd been feeling stressed. It had perched on his dashboard ever since. I chuckled at the photo and texted back:

> My mental health is DANGLING by a thread.

Gabe replied:

> Dangles doesn't seem too worried.

It was a full moon that night, and I went with Gabe's suggestion to bring the medicine into a ceremony. It was a way to transform the decision into a healing ritual, rather than the grasping-for-anything feeling I'd been carrying.

Back at my altar that evening, I closed my eyes and relaxed my body with deep breaths. I began to have that familiar sensation, as if a door had opened inside of me and I was dropping through it.

I called in the elements, my ancestors, and the Akashic Records guides and guardians into the space. I asked for a deeper understanding of what was happening with me, and to find alignment with taking the medication.

Soon, the response came in the form of meditative visions.

I saw the image of two snakes. The first was a garter snake, with skin a shiny emerald green. I knew this type of snake represented healing and the green shoots of new growth. It danced around the room in my mind's eye, its movement bright and energetic.

Next came a black cobra, its head and upper back wide and outstretched like a scaled hood, yellow eyes gleaming. It moved toward me slowly, with great ceremonial reverence. I had seen cobras in other ceremonies and knew they often symbolized family protection, rapid change, and the activation of great power.

But they can also symbolize death.

I felt the representation of all of these things—in the most neutral way, like a witness. It was true I was in a period of release. It was true I needed to confront darker feelings and aspects of myself.

I began to feel the energy of the cobra move through my head.

There are energies within your body that must shed.
There are beliefs within your mind you must release.
*Everything that must change, **will** change.*

I relaxed into the experience of my thoughts dissolving. Maybe this was what antidepressants could be like. I felt the snakes calling me to attention once again:

*Make your declarations. **Decide!***

Decide how you will move through the world and what you will truly commit to.

I started to feel sharp, clear, nearly caffeinated. I moved closer to the candlelight, grabbed a notebook and pen, and felt the truth of what I wanted pouring through my hand onto the page. No more drama. No more confusion. No more worrying about everything and everyone else.

It was time to remember who I was.

How much I *had* already created.

How much I could *still* create.

Through this ceremony, a new agreement with my life was being written. In rapid succession, the words flowed: my desires for my next home, my career, my relationships, my mental and physical health. The boundaries I would commit to with myself and with others. The declarations I would follow through on and the books I wanted to write.

I could feel my desire to live beginning to shine through the dark thoughts as I exhaled deeply. I felt powerful. *Yes.* These were the next steps to my life. It reminded me of what my former business coach had said to me just a few days earlier:

"You've simply forgotten your magnificence, darling."

During that conversation, I had been weepy and exasperated. But now, with the crisp words of my intentions written in front of me, the candle shadows dancing on the page, I felt a spark of hope.

If that's all it had been, I was ready to remember.

I put down my notebook and pen. I shook one tiny oval pill from the slim orange bottle and swallowed it.

The next morning, I woke up with a sense of *something*. I was still feeling the powerful reverberations of the ceremony, but once again, it lived alongside the dense layers of fatigue.

It was a Saturday so I stayed in bed, swaddled in my blanket as gray clouds rolled in from the beach; a storm announcing itself.

I pulled several books into bed with me. Anne, a longtime friend from Chicago—and Gabe's right-hand woman in his company—was one of the most diligent people I knew. Once she'd heard about my swollen neck, she overnighted me three heavy books on Hashimoto's Disease.

Maybe this is all in my thyroid? I thought.

I read for about an hour, then felt an even bigger wave of exhaustion fall over me. It was unyielding, and I surrendered, letting myself fall back asleep.

Three hours later, my phone rang. It was Gabe. I picked it up, put it on speaker, and answered in a voice thick with sleep.

He sounded upbeat. I could hear the steady slap of his sneakers and the mechanical wheeze of a treadmill.

"I'm at the gym," he said. "Just gonna let myself trust what the doctor said. Push through the anxiety and start *really* training again. I'm so excited to get back to basketball!"

Basketball had always been a love of Gabe's. A lifelong Knicks fan, he'd always played, but when the taller boys were picked over him in high school, he moved on to town leagues and eventually became a coach. For decades, he'd maintained a regular pickup game at the YMCA; known for his sharp defense and quiet prowess on the court.

More recently, finding his way through the dizziness and fear, he had channeled that passion into Qigong—something that grew physical strength, but not the heart-pumping kind.

That day my brother was in the mood to chat, so I listened. But the longer the conversation went on, the more I drifted. It was hard to hear him over the treadmill. But beyond that, it began to feel like we were in two different worlds.

As he spoke, I thought:

I am starving, and the only food I need is sleep—more and more and more. I am covered in fog, in darkness. I am a million miles away. I cannot cut through it. I just have to surrender.

After about fifteen minutes, Gabe said he'd catch me later and that he would send some funny pics from what was sure to be a dramatic Easter gathering at our aunt's house in Miami Beach.

"Okay, love you," I said, my voice groggy, before drifting back to sleep.

I'm grateful there were a million other phone calls and conversations when I wasn't drowning in fatigue. When I had said all I would've wanted to say to him, and more.

And I'm still glad that something in me was awake enough to pick up the phone that day.

APRIL, 2019: LOS ANGELES, CA

THE LAST SUPPER

$\mathcal{T}$he next afternoon, I slowly walked up the steps to the side door, arriving home from a friend's Easter Sunday gathering. Gabe, as promised, had sent some amusing snaps from the holiday at Aunt Rosemary's.

The next afternoon, I slowly walked up the steps to the side door, arriving home from a friend's Easter Sunday gathering. Gabe, as promised, had sent some amusing snaps from the holiday at Aunt Rosemary's.

Our aunt, Dad's sister, lives in Miami Beach in a grand old white house with dramatic pillars known as *The Hidden Arches*. She bought it in the 1980s with her second husband, Steven, a charismatic and posh Portuguese man with red hair and a disarming smile. They had just begun making big plans for their life there when he tragically died in his sleep, only a few years into their happy marriage.

Since then, Aunt Rosemary had remained in the house, keeping many of the designs and details just as she and Steven had chosen them, expecting a lifetime. After our grandfather's passing, our glamorous grandmother Connie, known as the Silver Fox for her charm, sharp wit, and *perfectly* set silver hair, came to live there too. Her beautiful bedroom, with its dramatic drapes and elegant terra cotta tones, still stood as it had before her passing years earlier.

We missed her crackling humor, the epic storytelling that could hold a room, and the sound of her singing in the kitchen and the smell of her famous meatballs simmering on the stove or signature dessert—a lemon meringue pie —cooling on the counter. But in a house layered with so many memories, the feeling of her presence lingered.

The back doors opened to lush palm trees, white wicker patio furniture, and a Spanish-tiled swimming pool, all backing up to a historic Miami Beach golf course. Inside were silver platters, fine china, and overhead fans that had been slowly rotating since the 1990s. The walls were covered with photos of family, friends, and the variety of Cocker Spaniels Aunt Rosemary had owned and treated with immense loving care over the years.

The surviving members of her animal brood included a twenty-year-old black cat named Minky, a massive collection of colorful and surprisingly friendly tropical aquarium fish, and the only two non-Spaniel dogs she'd ever owned: Marco Polo, an elderly chihuahua and solemn protector of the house, and Reina, a perpetually jolly and plump terrier who wore a diamond-encrusted bow on her head.

Somehow, this flash of glamor incensed Marco, who was occasionally caught trying to paw it out of Reina's fur. It was as if he knew she had been adopted when *he* had been mistakenly declared dead after running away from the vet.

At the time, my aunt was devastated and held a stately back-yard funeral for Marco. The next day, it was discovered the drowned dog my cousin had gone to recover hadn't, in fact, been Marco Polo—though he looked nearly identical. A cryptic phone call responding to the original *Lost Dog* flyers and a short drive later revealed the prodigal son had returned. Frail and skinny as a twig but very much alive, and still wandering the mean streets of Miami near the veterinary clinic where he had escaped six weeks earlier.

When Aunt Rosemary arrived, Marco eyed her suspiciously—semi-feral from his rustic adventure—but sprinted into her lap after she whispered a greeting in Spanish, just like his groomer always did.

Ever the animal lover, my aunt took comfort in knowing that the anonymous dog had received a memorial fit for royalty, while her beloved Marco was now safely back home. As the long-standing alpha of *The Hidden Arches*, Marco had been understandably both mortified and offended at the canine replacement. But over the years, he and Reina had come to a civil understanding. Reina adored him and Marco stoically tolerated her, even sharing the same perch on the staircase.

Aunt Rosemary had run a stock trading business from her home for many years and was known for her formal salons and holiday parties; a colorful who's who of eccentric and powerful long-time residents of the Beach. Any given event might include local city council members, the friar of St. Joseph's Church, a former attorney aged 101 in a smart purple suit with a rotating staff of nurses, an exotic animal veterinarian regularly flown in by Saudi royalty, and the French gardener with an elegant accent and supreme green thumb, who helped my aunt cultivate her famous rows of tomatoes, pineapples, and orchids.

That day, Gabe had sent me a short video of Gerard—a bar piano player, singer, and on-and-off fixture of *The Hidden Arches* social scene—playing with great flourish in the downstairs salon, surrounded by light blue satin brocade sofas. According to Gabe, Gerard had been forgiven for previous incidents and was back in the fold.

It had been decades since I'd seen this man in person, but his memory remained in our regular rotation of phrases we'd yell at each other without warning just to make the other laugh.

"I LOVE A PIANO!"

I texted back in all caps, referencing his signature theme song.

Gabe also sent a photo of Aunt Rosemary herself—the consummate hostess—six feet tall in flats, hair in a neat bun, smiling broadly and wearing her favorite necklace, a sapphire-adorned cross. She stood in front of a dining table stacked with cakes, pies, and filled Easter baskets, each stitched with every attendee's name, adult and child alike. On her head: tall white bunny ears. In her hand: an enormous silver knife, poised to slice into an elaborately frosted carrot cake.

Behind her was her son and most comedic nemesis, my cousin Arthur. In a single glance, I read the scene. Art knew exactly how funny the bunny ears plus giant knife *plus* Martha Stewart vibes looked—and he also knew Aunt Ro was completely unaware. So, he stood behind his mother, out of her view, with his pastel pink polo shirt and gleaming Rolex, grinning maniacally, eyes wide, as if it were an Easter-themed slasher flick gone wrong.

Oh boy. Everyone's up to their usual, I see

I texted, then slipped my phone into my purse and walked through the door into our own Easter gathering.

The savory smell of garlic, herbs, and sizzling beef hit me instantly. Kimiko stood at the stove, smiling over a pot of boiling potatoes, while her son moved around the living room setting up chairs.

"I decided to make Shepherd's Pie," she said. "It's the first episode of Season Eight of *Game of Thrones*. Ricky's here to watch, and Nia's coming over, and Mel and Kyle are coming up, too."

Nia was one of my oldest local friends. We'd met over a decade ago at one of her energy healing workshops back in Chicago. She was my teacher for a time, before becoming one of my dear friends. She and Kimiko had since struck up a friendship of their own.

Mel and Kyle were our downstairs neighbors; siblings a few years apart who hadn't grown up in the same household but were now living together in Venice to deepen their connection. We shared a backyard that, over the past couple of years, had become the setting for countless bonfires and late-night laughter. I loved their company, and the way their bond echoed the sibling closeness that meant so much in my own life.

They were moving out tomorrow. Mel was heading to Colorado, and Kyle to a new place in L.A. It was time. Plus, we were all increasingly concerned about the mold situation and the landlord's poor handling of it, which had sped up their plans.

Since they'd be gone the next day, I was glad we'd have one final hang as a house.

"Awesome," I said, half-joking. "It's the Last Supper."

I felt happy, and even happier to know that I could still feel that.

As we settled around the living room with bowls of mashed potatoes, herbed carrots and beef, and the epic opening credits of *Game of Thrones* began, a text came through from Gabe:

> I just got you a session with Pang. I told her how you were feeling this week. She's waiting for you on Zoom.

Pang was one of Gabe's most trusted Qigong teachers. As he had deepened his study, both as a student and practitioner, he worked with her weekly. She lived in China and guided him in perfecting his physical technique and five-organ sound healing practice.

One of the Qi methods Gabe had learned involved gently circling the area over the heart while breathing deeply—a movement he often did now, both intentionally and absentmindedly. He had suggested I try it too. But I hadn't been able to remember, let alone commit.

I set down my steaming bowl with disappointment, hesitant to miss the show and time with my friends. But after the week I had just put him through, I wouldn't dare argue. Gabe had stayed calm through it all, but I was sure I had scared him.

I told my friends I'd be back in a half hour, and quietly shut my bedroom door. There was no getting out of it now—which, perhaps, had been his aim.

I logged into the Zoom link and saw Pang, with her neat black bob and starched white t-shirt, sitting in a perfectly straight posture.

"Okay, we begin," she said in a pleasing Chinese accent and no-nonsense tone.

Pang wasn't phased by hearing I was entering something that felt like a true mental health crisis- a secret I had only shared with Gabe. Through her lens, everything was simply energy in the Qi field. And *anything* could be reoriented with the right practice.

After 30 minutes of methodical movement, guided breath, and visualization, I was already feeling lighter. We ended the session with the same heart massage Gabe had been gently urging me to try.

"This one has many a purpose," she said. "It will help with the want-to-die feelings. It helps a broken heart."

I chuckled softly and told her Gabe had been asking me to do it for weeks.

Pang smiled knowingly. "Sometimes we need to hear it from someone else."

Later that night, I walked Nia to her car. The wind whipped through the palm trees and her wavy blonde hair, while the tide crashed in the distance. It had been a good night with friends.

I told her about the climactic week and my decision to take antidepressants through ceremony. I knew she would understand;

her own path had led her to this work, too. I felt almost enthusiastic about the plan, and Nia met me there with the cheer of someone truly devoted to healing.

"It's funny," I said. "Now I can be honest that it's been like something has been haunting me; this *heavy* feeling. And I just know in my *bones* I'm finally going to confront it."

But the truth was, I had no idea just how confronted I would be.

APRIL, 2019: LOS ANGELES, CA

THE WORST THING EVER

I woke up the next morning to my phone buzzing, announcing a missed call. I opened one eye to check the time. It was 7:30 a.m., and I realized with disappointment that the heavy exhaustion was still there. Lately any relief I'd find the night before, no matter how profound, seemed to burn away with the morning sun.

The caller tried again. I looked at my phone.

It was Cousin Art in Miami Beach. He could be in any variety of moods and up to any variety of shenanigans. I wasn't ready. Not at 7:30 a.m.

I tried to psych myself up in my head:

Monday morning. We can do this!

First, I needed to pull myself into some version of physical and emotional alertness before a video call with a colleague. I began the practice Pang had taught me during our Qigong session the night before, praying that with each repetition, something would snap me out of this rut and back into my old self.

The phone buzzed again. It was Art—again.

I reasoned I'd try him later; it couldn't possibly be *that* important. The calls stopped.

Five minutes later, I was massaging my chest, the final step of the practice.

Help me heal this heavy heart, I prayed.

That's when Mom called. And I knew from experience that if I didn't answer, she really *would* keep calling. So this time, I picked up.

"Hi Mom, I have a meeting about to start, I will call—"

"No, Alee," she cut me off. "Whatever it is, it doesn't matter."

There were a few moments of silence, and I could feel her steadying herself.

What was wrong now?

"Today, the worst thing that could ever happen to our family has happened," she began, in an oddly formal tone.

As I recognized the beginning of yet another family crisis, my body went into the mode it always did when shit was going down. I became incredibly calm and present. Usually my brain would follow suit, but this time, my mind raced:

What would be the worst thing ever? Who could have died?

Even when it was really bad, Mom had never called it **The Worst Thing Ever.** I thought back to what I now realized might have been frantic rather than just insistent calls from Arthur.

Mom took a breath and began again.

"Alee, Gabe was on the treadmill in his building this morning."

Oh, shit. The stupid doctor was wrong. Pushing on the treadmill was a bad idea.

"Something happened to his heart while he was walking on it"

Okay, so the valve damage was worse than they thought. I wonder what hospital he's in. This is bad, but it's not the worst thing, right?

"And... and he died."

Those last words were spoken in a strangely light tone that felt almost translucent, without any grip. Like Mom couldn't believe they were coming out of her mouth. Like her brain could barely compute what she was saying.

Shock registered through my body like electricity. And then, almost instantly, a swift breeze of denial.

Nope.
They can bring him back.
*He must have **just** died, so they can jolt his chest with—whatever those things are called—and restart his heart. They can still bring him back. They just need to do it now, while there's still time.*
Someone needs to get to the hospital and tell them what to do.

While my brain spun its fantasy outside of reality, my body already knew the truth.

As if removed from myself, I heard my voice shouting a continuous, steady stream of *"NO!"*

Mom's voice began to shudder into a deep cry. I could hear another woman sobbing in the background. It sounded like her friend, Barbara. She must have raced over there.

"He's dead. I'm so sorry, Alee, but it's true. He's gone."

As if in a trance, my legs took me out of bed and walked me stiffly around my room. I was wearing the lavender flannel pajamas I had given to my grandmother one winter. I had taken them back to start wearing as a comfort item just three months ago, when I cleaned out her closet after she died.

We had *just* lost Bubbie.

How could Gabe be gone now, too?

I stumbled out of my bedroom into the living room. My pastel pink sherpa mat—the one I used for Kundalini yoga—was still laid out on the floor by the coffee table.

I threw myself down on my hands and knees and began to sob.

The mat was soft under my palms. I had spent so many hours here, praying, chanting, exerting myself. Trying to be better. Always trying to be better.

Especially this past year, when everything had felt so wrong.

All those early mornings, waking up at dawn for practice.

Until recently, when I could barely wake up at all.

Those hours spent in the dark, getting on this mat and doing the kriyas my teacher said could move mountains and ignite miracles. Desperately praying to do enough, to *be* enough. Praying for the bottom of this down to finally drop out and bring me somewhere else.

But now, this mat would hold the tortured shock and agony of my grief as its final act of service.

I knew I would have to throw it out, just like I had thrown out my all-time favorite T-shirt after I happened to be wearing it the day Dad died. It was perfectly weathered, a soft dusty peach, and afterwards it had a splash of his blood on the front pocket. For about six hours, it was comforting to wear. And then, it had to be thrown out. There was no way I could see it as a shirt I'd ever wear again.

The cries coming out of me now were long and ancient. They came from a place inside me that had never been heard before. A place only the loss of my brother could summon.

I looked up and saw Kimiko in the doorway. She'd heard me yelling and came running from her room.

"What's wrong?!" she asked, alarmed.

I could barely breathe, but I gasped out, "Gabe died."

She dropped down onto the ground with me and, without asking anything else, began to cry too.

Although I was not alone, the next thought that came to me was that I couldn't be here without Gabe, because he was the only person I had ever completely trusted in this world. He had been here first, and he had always been here for me. My shock and grief said that there was no safety here without my brother.

My mind flashed back to that session with Morgan, just before I got on the plane to visit him for the last time.

I am afraid of someone else dying, my unconscious had revealed at the time.

Now I understood. Now I knew why I'd felt so despondent about being alive this past week, and why I had confided in my brother about it. I would have **never** wanted to leave a world where Gabe still lived. But he wouldn't be living here anymore.

And some part of me already knew that. I hadn't just been grieving my past fears for him over the last month. I had been grieving what was about to happen, while he was still here to comfort me. It was clear now. I had been calling out to go with him, so desperate to remain in a shared reality with my best friend.

I curled into a ball; my body tightening in terror, my mind beginning to take stock of just how *much* suffering awaited me. I still remembered the years of misery after Dad's death; the lingering, visceral grief. All the bittersweet moments. The tears. The going without. Having the best father of all and still becoming a girl with daddy issues.

But we had made meaning of it. We had carried on. It was all still in the "right" order, sad as it was. He had died just after turning 53. So young—I hadn't fully understood just how young that was, when at the time I was only twenty.

I squeezed myself tighter.

I can't do this again. Not for Gabe. And not without Gabe.

I don't want to live in a place where this could have happened to him.

That's when I realized my phone was still nearby, because I heard my mother screaming my name. I picked it up, put her on speaker, and choked out the only words I had:

"Mom, I can't do this. I really can't do this without him. I know everyone thinks I'm this nice spiritual healer person who likes people, but actually I *hate* everyone."

Tears poured down my hot, swollen face as I continued hysterically,

"I'm only just now realizing that *I've never liked anyone.* I've actually only ever been *tolerating* people, I swear. I hate everyone in the world besides him. I can't live here if he's gone."

There was a pause, and then Mom spoke in a low, calm voice.

"Listen to me, Alee. You can't kill yourself. Because if you do, *I'm* going to kill *myself*, and then the whole family is gone."

She took a breath. Her voice sharpened.

"We are going to get through this. I have no idea how we're going to get through this yet, but I know Gabe will be here. And Dad. And Bubbie too. They're going to help us do it. I can feel them already."

I felt Mom's fierce, powerful knowing and I snapped back into presence. She had always said that when Gabe was born, she looked down and immediately recognized she had given birth to an angel. At that moment, the decision was made to scrap the original name and call him Gabriel, like the archangel.

He would be with us.

After Mom and I hung up to begin whatever this day would require, I started tracking the spiritual threads, as my brother and I always did.

It was the morning after Easter: a day of rebirth.

It was *Earth Day*—and Gabe had loved this world, had been in service to its healing.

Gabe had only one tattoo, which he got after Dad died.

Three large black numbers down his spine:

2 – 2 – 7.

It was intended as a fusion of Dad's special number, 22, and Gabe's birthday, the 27th.

But now I saw it meant something more.

Gabe was born on January 27th, 1981.

He died on April 22nd, 2019.

2 – 2 – 7.

The tattoo was the intersection of his earthly birth and death days, placed down his spine—that physical center point between heaven and earth, between the physical and energetic body.

His new apartment had also been #22.

Gabe's spirit had orchestrated the way he would continue to support me, even now. The "Last Supper" with friends. The session with Pang. It had all ensured that my heart would already be open and in active healing when the worst news of my life arrived. Now I understood why he had kept telling me to do that heart-healing practice.

His conscious self hadn't known, but his spirit had.

I looked down at my phone, my eyes still blurry with tears.

In two hours, I had an appointment with Dale, a numerologist I'd first met through Gabe. For the past couple of years he had worked with us, and with many of our friends and clients, deciphering life paths through the language of numbers. The session had been booked two months earlier, but of course it was scheduled for today. Of course.

Everything was insane, but as I zoomed out, I could track the threads, see the design and feel the invitation to trust.

To trust the experience.

To trust Gabe, as I always had.

When it was time for my call with Dale, I sat on my bedroom floor, my back against the wall. I was damp with adrenaline and emotional exertion. I dialed his number to start our meeting and, as soon as he answered I said,

"Dale, I have something to tell you that's going to be very intense to receive, so I think you should sit down and take a breath."

He responded quizzically, and I continued, steeling myself.

"This morning Gabe passed away. It was something with his heart, but we're still figuring out what exactly happened."

I held for a beat, hearing his shaky gasp. I felt the shock move across the line.

I would make this type of call many times; reaching out to those Gabe loved, those who loved him, those who had walked with him through healing and his life. I would become familiar with that stunned inhale. With the silence. Holding for the exhale, offering the grace we all need when an unthinkable event has just been spoken into existence.

Had it really been *me* taking in the same information, feral with grief on my sherpa mat just two hours ago?

I knew I would be in that state again. But for now, I was locked into the mission of the day:

Notify the people. Pack a suitcase for the most surreal trip of my life. Survive another red-eye to Miami.

And, in this moment, connect with Dale for this fated meeting.

It took a few minutes for him to absorb the news. But once he did, he agreed with me: We had always been meant to meet on this day. And we should still have the session. Dale began again, his rich, broadcaster-like voice steadying me.

"The numerology of Gabe's current year is also the numerology of his life path: 11/2. *Deeply* spiritual. This is a master number. It means you are here for a very clear and powerful assignment. But when you're done—you're done. That's it. It means the life will be truly impactful, but not *necessarily* long, if it's not part of the mission. Sometimes *when* you leave becomes a part of your impact."

I closed my eyes and felt myself jolt into spiritual connection with Gabe's energy. For the first time since my world imploded that morning, I left the logistics along with the primal experience of learning of his death. I joined him in the ethereal.

From this space I could feel two distinct aspects of my brother.

There was the soul part of him, the one that had known and guided it all: getting him to the apartment in Miami, making sure almost every one of his close friends, as well as Mom and I, had visited during his nine short weeks there. Nine, the number of completion. Then the doctor's appointment and dying the way he did. I could already sense it would allow for a deeper karmic resolution.

That part of him felt solid, strong, and trusting.

Dale paused, then said:

"I feel Gabe here with us. His soul has left the body. And he's certainly *very* disappointed. He didn't want to go yet. He just can't believe this had to happen."

And yes, that was the second part I could feel: the human personality. Confused and stunned as he realized that what he had feared and fought off had finally come for him. He had died.

I breathed in, bringing this part of his energy into my heart. I felt so sad for him. I was desperate to take away his fear, and Dale sensed it too.

"Let's hold space for his journey now," he said gently.

Together we envisioned Gabe's energy field filled with love, support, and gratitude. Through tears, I said:

"Thank you for everything, Gabe."

As we meditated, the vision of his personality began to shift. I could feel my brother remembering his beloved Qigong practice, realizing *this* was why he had devoted himself so earnestly in his final years.

Not to save his body from death, but to live inside of it in his strongest, most empowered form. And then, when the time came, to return to the formless with that same grace. I saw him surrounded by waves of golden, vibrating light. He held a glowing gold orb in his hands and then stretched his arms wide. The light was everywhere. He smiled.

I sat in stillness, relaxing into the relief of the vision. Dale was connected to the same energy.

"He's okay now," he said, voice soft. "Your brother knows what to do."

We sat in silence. Then Dale's voice became more vigorous again.

"A few more things. Gabe wants me to tell you: *Now you really have a book to write!* It's going to be your time to tell the story you're meant to. And of course, he's going to help you do it."

I swallowed hard, the silent tears continuing. Just two nights ago, in the snake ceremony, I'd felt the dream of finally writing it. It felt both true and impossibly far away.

After we hung up, I saw an incoming call from Gabe's best friend, James.

"Hi," I answered softly.

"Okay, I'm bringing Sean on—one sec."

It was a three-way call with James and Sean, Gabe's closest friends from home. They had been through all of it with our family. They had grieved our dad, who they loved like a second father. They drove me to school during Gabe's chemo, shaved their heads to match him, and wore ridiculous dragon and snake temporary tattoos on their bald heads to make us laugh. They were roommates in college, and beyond that, they were family.

Their brother had just died, too.

We all got on the line. And finally, I didn't have to say a word. I could just breathe and cry.

"Oh, Al," Sean said, and his own tears began.

There had been talk of them flying across the country to bring me to Florida; Mom was worried I couldn't manage alone. But that seemed crazy. I just wanted us all to get to Miami. Being together was the lifeline now.

We hung up to start our travel plans.

I looked out my window and saw that sunset was nearing. The very last day of Gabe's human life was ending, and I needed to mark it.

I saw the white roses from the full moon ceremony on the kitchen table. Gently, I slid them from the vase and walked barefoot to the ocean. I set the roses on the sand and closed my eyes, beginning Gabe's Qigong practice.

When I told Pang earlier that day that he had passed, at first she hadn't believed me.

"How could this happen to his big, strong heart?" she cried.

She told me to carry on his practice, if I could.

"There was a specific kind of energy coming to Earth through

Gabe's body, through this movement. You can continue his work by letting it come through your body."

I started right there on the beach, practicing the Wisdom Qi Gong series Gabe had most loved, which was called *Awaken Vitality*.

Afterward, I picked up the roses and scattered the petals into the waves as the burnt-colored sun disappeared below the horizon.

Today is the last day of life as we have known it.

Whatever I thought had been going on...was **nothing** compared to the reality now.

And then I remembered the Akashic message I received in the ocean on my last day with Gabe:

You are about to be tested beyond anything you have ever experienced.

I couldn't have imagined it would be this. But I had been told that whatever it was, I wouldn't be able to prevent it. I would have to accept it.

I thought of what I had so often explained to clients in Akashic sessions:

"This energy is a mentorship.
It's about receiving, not taking.
You don't insist on what you want to know.
You receive what is actually *needed* for your current journey."

Still, I saw now where I had misunderstood. Where I had thought my spiritual practice could give me the strength to *control* the moment rather than simply the grace to *meet* it.

That old idea faded with every fallen petal.

Once my hands were empty, I felt pulled toward the water and waded in fully dressed. The ocean was still brisk from spring, only welcoming to wet-suited surfers. But right then, the cold felt soothing. It was something my numb body could feel.

I floated up to my neck. A large wave crested, and I ducked beneath it, letting the saltwater meet my tears.

When I returned to the shore soaked, my wet clothes heavy on my body, Kimiko was waiting. Her face was soft. She had followed me down and filmed from the sand, so that I would have the memory.

"Check it out—Gabe was with you the whole time," she said, handing me her phone.

In the video, an iridescent blue orb shimmered around me, following my every motion.

It was beautiful. I was grateful. But it was also surreal. This morning my brother had been a person, and now he was just light.

We walked back to the house, where a group of friends waited at the front door.

"We're here to pack you up for the red-eye and feed you!" Lauren declared, hoisting a barbecue chicken in a clear bubble container above her dark curls.

Lauren had been one of my best friends since Chicago. We were neighbors for years. Celebrations, heartaches—we'd walked through it all. We also both had that Sicilian gene, so we were bringing food either way.

While I changed into sweats, my friends crammed around our tiny kitchen table, perched on folding chairs, yoga balls, and rocking chairs. They passed around the bags of chicken, coleslaw, and baked beans.

I had no appetite, but watching them packed in while eating drumsticks warmed my broken heart. They had walked right into our kitchen and into my pain, not knowing what it would be like. I was so grateful for their presence.

After dinner, I pulled out my suitcase while friends sat on my bed. I froze, unsure what to pack.

What do you bring for the worst trip of your life?

With their encouragement, I weakly tossed in a bathing suit, a hoodie and some yoga pants. I didn't think we'd be doing a funeral at this point, but found a black dress anyway.

When it was time, everyone loaded into three cars and drove me caravan-style to the airport. I didn't even have to ask.

During the drive, it felt like Gabe was sending songs through the 1980s radio station: *"I'll Be Watching You,"* by Sting and *"Don't You Forget About Me"* by Simple Minds.

The security line blurred by as I took the first Xanax of my life and felt the chemical reaction quickly blanket my brain.

My first antidepressant and sedative in the same 48 hours. I've gone mainstream.

I thought it would be an easy flight—surely my guardian angels would clear the way on the *worst day ever*—but apparently, they had other assignments.

The plane was sweltering, the AC was broken and the crowd was loud. And then—surprise!—there was a 3 a.m. layover in South Carolina.

"Folks, we're way off schedule. If you were connecting to Miami, you've missed that flight."

*I didn't even know there was a connection. Wait, who booked this flight? How is a red-eye with a **layover** even a thing?*

The Xanax and adrenaline was wearing off. My brain felt wrung out like a rag. I wandered toward the gate and came across a row of massive white rocking chairs. Half were filled with solemn strangers eating Auntie Anne's pretzels. It felt like a fever dream.

Are these people or ghosts? And where did they all get pretzels in the middle of the night?

I sat down and scrolled Facebook to see Gabe's profile page had a new post.

> I can't believe this…Only the good die young. You were a real one, bro. I'll always remember your fire on the basketball court <3

*What?! How does **he** know?*

This was an old pal from Gabe's high school years, but there were much closer friends who still hadn't gotten the news.

I DM'd the guy, asking him to delete the post for now. Then I saw a comment in Gabe's Facebook group for his company's coaching program:

> "Is it true? I heard Gabe Hoffman died?!
> Some kind of brain aneurysm?"

The thread ballooned with doctors both speculating and lamenting. I started to reply, but stopped myself. I texted Anne. She would handle it tomorrow.

Primal rage bubbled up in me when I saw all of these words on the screen; unverified information about something so raw and vulnerable that I was so desperate to protect. It felt as if the worst thing I could have ever fathomed was already becoming an info-bite; something of note to discuss with people who weren't even *close* with Gabe.

Yes, the love would pour in. Yes, much of it would be beautiful. So many people would surely be sharing from their heart—*everyone* loved Gabe. But in that moment, it felt like all of it was being taken from us; including the telling of it. There was still so much we didn't even know.

By morning, I arrived at Arthur's house in Miami Beach empty-handed. Somewhere in the chaos of multiple airports, my suitcase had vanished to the ethers. Probably with the pretzel ghosts. I collapsed on the couch. Arthur and his wife, Ali, sat on stools at the breakfast bar, wide-eyed and wired.

"So," I croaked "What *happened?*"

Arthur stood up and began to pace. Tall and trim, his gestures were sharp and agitated as he spoke. He explained that the building had called yesterday morning; my brother had listed him as the emergency contact. They told Art there had been a "cardiac event" in the gym, and Gabe had been taken to the hospital.

"I thought he was okay, just resting in a room. But when I got there..." His voice cracked. "They gave me that look — the one where you just *know* it's not good. They said they'd been trying to revive him since the gym. But he never came back."

I stared at Arthur. His angular jaw, just like our grandfather's, was clenched, and the whites of his pale eyes were reddened with tears. Gabe was his person, too.

Just then, the front door burst open.

Sean, lanky and windblown, stepped inside, wearing Nikes just like my brother's. Behind him was James, solid and steady with his auburn curls peeking from beneath a baseball cap. They looked as shell-shocked as any of us, but their familiar faces still brought a wave of comfort.

Whatever the rest of this horrible week would hold, at least we would go all through it together.

APRIL, 2019: MIAMI BEACH, FL

THE APARTMENT

*A*fter talking a little more with Art, I headed out to Gabe's apartment with James and Sean. The three of us would be spending the week there.

We arrived at the vast white entrance of the building. Only weeks—and in James' case, just *days*—earlier, we had all visited him here. The big glass doors framed by palm trees, once so welcoming, now looked foreboding.

The front lobby, with its natural modern décor and chilly, spa-scented air, had felt elegant and refreshing the last time I was here. Now it felt like I had entered the barbed-wire gates of a prison with no exit.

We walked past the front desk; James and Sean each took one of my hands as I began to cry softly. By then, the staff and residents had already been told what had happened in the community gym. As we passed, everyone in the lobby stared at us with sadness and pity, brows knitting as they drew in sharp breaths, bracing against the weight of it.

As we took the elevator up, I thought back to my first ride. Gabe had held my suitcase, still on his headset for a business meeting. So much in motion, and so much still unfinished. As we glided to the 11th floor I blurted out,

"Well, this is fucking surreal."

We walked out and rounded the outdoor corridor. The same expanse of blue sky, Miami high-rises and turquoise water; just as I'd seen it that first morning nine weeks ago.

But this time, there were no manatees.

I turned the handle and opened the door. A hushed silence fell over us, as the sudden realization hit that we were entering sacred ground. The last moments of Gabe's life were encapsulated here. No one had been inside since he'd died, just over twenty-four hours ago.

I felt the heavy responsibility of entering his private space, knowing he hadn't expected anyone else would see it. There was a striking vulnerability in that. How does anyone leave their apartment on a busy Monday morning, assuming they're just heading downstairs for a quick workout?

We all felt the need to witness whatever remained of Gabe's aliveness here—and at the same time, the desire to protect his privacy. This was our final chance to do that for him. The urgency of both things collapsed into a push-pull in my chest.

There was still so much to sort through: his apartment, his phone and computer, his New York storage unit. But for now, it was just about opening this door.

We walked slowly through the apartment, retracing his final steps. On the sofa lay the smiling sloth throw blanket I had insisted he buy at Marshall's, to match Dangles. He'd resisted, calling it unnecessary, but by the end of my visit he was often snuggled in the blanket during moments of rest.

On the coffee table was the last book he had been reading—*The Art of War*, opened to Chapter Four: "Tactical Dispositions."

Beside it, a *Black Panther* mug held the remnants of his morning green tea. We had loved watching that movie during his surgery recovery, and bought the official merchandise mug set on the same Marshall's trip. *WAKANDA FOREVER* was printed across each one.

The mug reminded me of my favorite part of the visit with Gabe. Each morning, we would step outside to the outdoor terrace to perch on his new woven gray and white patio chairs that we had somehow crammed in the back of a rental car. We sat and sipped our morning beverages in those mugs, surrounded by his new tropical plants as we stared at the water in peaceful connection. For those two weeks, I cherished the time we could just hang out in the hopeful light of a new day.

In the bathroom, his toothbrush sat drying on the sink. A small pink spiral notepad lay beside it, entitled

Email for the Team

alongside a bulleted list written in Gabe's sharp, elongated handwriting.

In the bedroom, sunlight poured through the blinds onto his windowsill altar: a heart-shaped moonstone, glittering pyrite, a selenite wand with chakra-colored stones, and a glossy tiger's eye laced with gold and brown.

Above the bed was the same framed photograph of three African lions napping on each other that had always hung in his office back in New York.

"Well, he *did* make the bed," Sean joked, looking at the dark gray sheets and slightly rumpled comforter. "In his own mangle-mitts fashion."

The term—*mangle-mitts*—was a long-standing rib about Gabe's handiwork. Every paper item on his desk or in his wallet looked like it had about a thousand wrinkles, even if it was relatively new.

His pajama pants were on the floor, molded in the shape of legs, dropped perfectly over his slippers. It struck us all in a funny way, imagining how he must have stepped right out of them to change into gym clothes.

These tiny, silly details about Gabe's life were our inheritance. All three of us had lived with him; had known and been known by him, and observed his daily eccentricities, as he had ours. As we moved through each space in the apartment, we wept and chuckled, sometimes simultaneously. Our shared dark humor carried us through the process, while we pictured the way Gabe had been moving about during his last morning alive.

There was a sobering awareness that it was our final opportunity to lovingly tease Gabe in real-time. After this small passage of moments, it would only ever happen again as a bittersweet memory. We took in every detail possible.

I looked at the Scandinavian-style slippers on the bedroom floor again. They were a cloudy gray wool with dark blue thread, and another thing I had insisted he needed. The slippers were part of a set of a dozen pairs in various sizes that had come in a woven pouch. I remembered my sales pitch:

"You don't want people to wear shoes in the house, right? This can be the new vibe! Whenever someone visits, they take off their shoes and put on the guest slippers!"

At the time, he raised one eyebrow at me. "Woolen guest slippers? In *Florida?*"

But now I saw that the basket of slippers was by the front door, and the pair in his size were the ones in his bedroom. The fact that he was trying out this idea so earnestly—the way he tried everything—touched my heart. Tears started to stream down my face again.

I walked to the kitchen and opened the fridge. Stacked Tupperware containers held all the Easter food Aunt Rosemary had sent him home with: chestnut stuffing, baked ham with caramelized pineapple, asparagus. I could picture him grabbing a water bottle before the gym, eyeing the leftovers and looking forward to lunch.

Once we had walked through the apartment, the three of us sat quietly in the living room. The adrenaline of discovery wore off and the shocked despondence had returned.

At that moment, the door opened and Gabe's business partner Maskell bounded through, somehow magically holding my lost suitcase from the airport. It struck me like a Seinfeld episode, when Kramer would enter Jerry's apartment unexpectedly and add a new twist to the plot.

As usual, Maskell was a strong presence: six foot three, with a taste for boldly printed clothes inspired by his years in South Africa and annual pilgrimages to Burning Man. That day he wore a flamingo-print button-down in bright blue and pink, loose linen slacks, and weathered red Toms.

His wavy brown hair and slightly disheveled clothes suggested he had jumped out of bed and dashed to the airport in Costa Rica as soon as he heard the terrible news. Maskell's large brown eyes— so often sparkling and animated when he shared an idea in his lilting British accent—were now red-rimmed and heavy. The vividness of his outfit in contrast to the bleak situation offered a fleeting spark of levity, even as my heart broke for him.

Gabe and Maskell had met a decade earlier; both young and passionate disruptors in the field of functional medicine. Over time, they had built a successful business together called Evolution of Medicine, fulfilling many of the creative and professional visions they had once shared with me during late-night talks in those early days.

This next chapter was supposed to be their biggest yet, the one where they could ensure long-term stability for themselves and their team and the legacy of wonderful projects still to come. And now it was over—at least as the duo they had been.

Needing fresh air, the four of us walked to the café across the street from Gabe's building. Oliver's was a friendly little spot with bright orange awnings and big box fans that stirred the potted tropical plants in every direction. Mom texted to say she had arrived and would meet us there shortly.

My last meal with Gabe had been at this very place, along with Mom and our family friend Mark, just before I left for the red-eye flight back to L.A. I'd sipped a perfectly foamy cappuccino, and we'd gotten a little bit of everything that looked good, which was my brother's typical way of ordering. When the check came, he'd swiftly picked it up, as he often did.

"I'm so happy to have you all here at my new home," he said.

Later that night, he texted us three photos from the dinner: candid portraits of each of us when we weren't looking. The last way Gabe had seen us.

As we walked the short distance to the café, that sweet memory clashed with the sharp reality of our current moment. Four people, tethered together by him. But he was not here, and never would be again.

With that thought, a wave of horror moved through my body like black ink dissolving in water. It didn't matter where life had taken us over the years or how far apart we were geographically—I never felt alone, because of Gabe. He had always been here on Earth first. That was enough of a beacon to guide me out of whatever stress or fear I was feeling.

At least Gabe is my brother.

Now, I was beginning to realize I had never known the true depths of loneliness. But I was about to find out. For the first time in my 35 years of life, I would be on my own, unmoored in a way I had never experienced. Gabe had been a constant presence, even across distance. He was my lifetime best friend and protector. And I had been his.

That understanding landed hard, and I felt a visceral sensation of being dropped. Whatever emotional tether had connected me to him and whatever way it anchored me in the world- it was gone. My knees buckled, and I fell onto the asphalt in the middle of the road.

Just as quickly, James and Maskell pulled me back up, each taking an arm and steadying me for the rest of the walk to Oliver's. My face contorted with grief. The security that had come with being Gabe's sister had disappeared; I now was in the world just as me. Surrounded by others, I felt unbearably alone.

Then Mom arrived. She was exhausted and stunned, but somehow still holding it together. Her deep resilience, called upon so many times, was here again. We hugged without speaking, both of us beyond tears. Her soulmate of a son was gone. And I, in my spiraling grief, wondered morbidly what it felt like to be left with only her more complicated daughter.

That night, I was back at the apartment with James and Sean. I had asked for these first nights to be just the three of us here, and I was grateful it was granted. We'd already worked out our sleeping setup: I'd take Gabe's bed, and James and Sean would crash in the living room on a blow-up mattress and the couch. It felt protective, like guards posted outside the gates of my healing cave.

In fact the two of them had served as a line of defense many times throughout our youth. They'd been part of the inner circle during both Dad's and Gabe's health journeys. My own high school and college friends didn't always know how to respond to what was happening, nor did I really know how to explain it. But James and Sean —three years older and directly involved with the situation—had made sure to show up for me.

I looked at them and realized Gabe left me with two honorary brothers, ones who had accepted that assignment long ago.

We sprawled across his bed with hip-hop playing softly in the background and small glasses of tequila over ice on the nightstand. Every so often, one of us would get up, pace, and speak aloud a thought or memory from the day. The others would respond. It was a familiar style of decompression; one we'd known since we were young.

From long afternoons at our house growing up, to their student housing at Quinnipiac, to their infamous post-grad house, "The Dude Dorm" in Huntington Village, where they lived with other hometown friends, and even later, when life scattered us into our separate adult worlds—we always returned to this way of being.

Still, up until now, my connection to James and Sean orbited around Gabe. While the two of them were just as close with each other, he had made the three of *us* siblings. While I'd spent time with each of them without my brother it had been rare, especially as we got older. Now, that would be the only way. The dynamic between us was warm and instinctual, like we had grown up in the same litter of puppies, but the nucleus was missing.

How would we relate now, without Gabe at the center?

I set down my glass of water and stood.

"This is insane. How could this happen? I still can't believe we are sitting in his room right now and he fucking *died*. He took better care of himself than anyone else. It's not right."

Sean nodded quietly. Then James stood, his brown eyes shimmering with tears. He exhaled and said:

"I think the reality none of us wanted to say is that sometimes, it felt like Gabe had been fighting for his life ever since he first got sick twenty years ago. It was intense. He had great years—really great years—but he was always looking for the next thing that would make him feel totally safe, once and for all. We all knew how hard he worked for that."

My whole being relaxed with his words. I didn't want to resist or make James wrong. I didn't need to list the evidence of Gabe's vitality, or argue that he'd been healthy. What was I trying to prove?

Yes, Gabe had been vibrant and strong. And he had also been working tirelessly to feel that way. Physically, emotionally, and spiritually. He had grown up with the story of our maternal grandfather dying at 38—what now turned out to be the same age as Gabe—and had watched our dad pass not long after his own remission. He'd been there for our Uncle Joel's death from cancer, a family member he was very close with. And, of course, he himself had endured aggressive treatments that never fully left him.

My brother didn't want to be identified with being sick. He wanted to focus on everything that came *afterwards*. The decades dedicated to understanding nutrition, spiritual practice and health technologies. A life where he was an understated but brilliant teacher, guide and ally.

Dammit, he had just *been* here—sipping his Chinese herbs while taking work calls, cooking kitchari for neighbors, laughing at funny videos before bed.

Until he wasn't.

By his thirties, he had built tight routines: the hours of Qigong, precise supplement schedules, carefully guarded habits. He didn't want people to see the effort, or to wonder if there was fear underneath the discipline. Most of the time, I didn't see it either. In my loyalty, I agreed not to look too closely. Like that night in the hospital with Dad, I had made a quiet vow to stay in the light.

But more recently, I had begun to notice changes in Gabe. I worried. I spoke to him about it, even shed a tear when the fear broke through. He seemed stressed, maybe even guilty for causing my concern. That in turn made me feel guilty for placing any weight on him. I just wanted him to be okay.

Gabe had made a vow of his own: never to live as if a doctor held more power over his survival than he himself did. Gabe didn't want to be defined as a sick person, not for himself and not for us. So most of the time, I kept my worries quiet. But sometimes, they found their way to the surface.

It had come up the year before, at a weekend training in San Francisco. I was staying in a house with friends, and they gently called me out for seeming subtly but often worried about the well-being of the group, especially the men.

"It truly feels life and death in the moment, to know everyone is okay," I admitted, my voice catching.

One of the guys stepped closer, placed his hands on my shoulders, and looked straight into my eyes.

"But Alee, it's *not* life or death anymore. That's just your old story. You've got to let it go."

I wanted to believe him, the way I always wanted to believe that my brother was safe; that my fear was just old residue, that the doctors had come back in at just the right time, and nothing bad could happen again.

But something did happen. The very thing we'd always half-braced for, the one we prayed could never catch up with Gabe again.

And we didn't have to deny it anymore.

APRIL, 2019: MIAMI BEACH, FL

THE LAST TIME

I heard the James and Sean call my name from Gabe's bedroom, and when I walked in, I saw multiple hangers of clothing draped over both of them: brightly colored polo shirts, crisp checkered button-downs, blue jeans in varying shades.

Sean leaned into the closet, hunting for pairs of Gabe's signature shoe, Nike Air Force Ones. For Sean's son Andrew's first birthday, Gabe had given the baby a tiny inaugural pair.

They moved through the closet with urgency, more clothing piling onto their arms, and I chuckled. It amazed me that in the middle of the worst days of my life, I could still smile.

"You *know* how your mom feels about clothes," Sean said.

"We need options," James added.

I laughed softly again, "Mom will like whatever we bring. Let's be real, she helped him pick out half of it anyway."

They were choosing the outfit Gabe would wear for the viewing; our final chance to see him before cremation. I felt my brother's energy with us, gently pulling us toward certain choices. In the end, we chose dark blue jeans, his favorite aqua-colored polo shirt, and dark gray Air Jordans. Sean added the tea tree toothpicks and protein bar Gabe always carried in his pockets. My cousin dropped the items off at the funeral home so we could return later, all together, to see him.

We took Gabe's car. I sat in the back while James and Sean were up front, windows down, hip-hop playing, the warm spring air rushing in. It was a ride like so many we'd taken since I was in eighth grade—in every way but one.

Curled up in the backseat, I looked down at my phone and opened Facebook. The next wave of posts had begun: tributes and announcements, including mine and Mom's. I had helped her upload it the night before. This was the new language of loss; a social media post was more important than a newspaper obituary. More immediate and more connected to the global community's ability to share.

Hundreds of comments and likes from people I knew well, those I hadn't seen in years or else didn't know at all. Everyone was sharing memories of my brother, screenshots of kind texts, gestures, and stories of the quiet support Gabe was always offering behind the scenes. It was overwhelmingly beautiful and painful. A blur.

As we were slowly unraveling what had really been happening with him physically, I saw now just how many people he'd been showing up and extending himself for. Everyone seemed think Gabe had been a special support or mentor *just* to them. The number felt endless.

All of that, on top of his intense workload, on top of everything going on with our family, and—I thought guiltily—on top of my recently leaning on him, too. I'd been worried about how hard he kept pushing himself during his recovery from surgery.

"Doesn't everyone realize what you're recovering from?" I snapped once back at Mom's, seeing him on a headset in a long business meeting about a week post-op, when he was still unable to walk.

The memory gave me a knot in my stomach and a dry throat.

Apparently, no one really *did* know what he was trying to recover from. Not even him.

We pulled into the funeral home parking lot and met the rest of the family. Aunt Rosemary wore a black mourning dress and looked somber. My cousin April was in a navy pantsuit. Mom wore a gauzy sundress in lavender and gray; not traditionally funeral, but reverent in her way. Her presence was calm and steady in the face of horror. She knew it was on her to set the tone.

The six of us stood there for a moment, just outside the door, knowing we were about to step into something that would never leave us.

Finally, Mom reached for the handle.

We entered the cool, quiet hallway of the funeral parlor. Zev, the young, plump funeral director with a full head of curls and oversized Andy Warhol-style glasses, was waiting. He led us toward the room where we would see Gabe, then took a deep breath before speaking.

"Gabe is ready for you . . . and honestly, he looks great. I mean, *phenomenal*. Better than most. We all thought he had such great style. And I see he and you guys are all wearing *these*!"

Zev held up his wrist and pointed to his father, the funeral home's owner, who lifted his own wrist. Just like us, they wore three stacked bracelets, each made from various round stones.

"We make them ourselves. Stringing them at night after work is very relaxing," the father said.

A soft wave of laughter moved through us, especially Mom, James, and Sean. It was the kind of slice-of-life moment that would've cracked Gabe and Dad up. It felt like they had guided us into it.

Zev's face became more serious.

"Ready?" he asked.

We were ready.

He opened the door and we filtered in slowly. The room was dimly lit with white lamps. A few large beige couches sat nearby, along with vases of white flowers arranged on glossy wooden tables. And in the corner, on a wheeled table, was Gabe. He wore the clothes we had chosen. The corner of the protein bar wrapper peeked from his jean pocket, a white blanket draped across his torso.

As I walked closer, I braced myself. This moment could comfort me—or it could traumatize me, terrify me, undo me completely—and I wouldn't know which until it happened.

I'd seen my father and grandparents' bodies after they'd passed. In those moments, they still looked like themselves. But I'd also seen Bubbie and others in open caskets, and sometimes it felt like looking at a mannequin. A likeness, but not exactly the person.

Seeing my brother fell somewhere in the middle.

My attention first landed on what was off. His face was still suntanned, his scruff neatly trimmed, but his lips were slightly tinged with blue. So were his fingers. There was a little bit of redness around his neck, and a small abrasion on his head and eyelid where he'd fallen. I winced at the thought of how hard his head must have hit the treadmill.

Then I remembered what his spirit had told me, during that first connection:

I didn't feel it after that.

It was faster than a finger snap.

Gabe's body was cold and his torso rigid. When my hand touched his chest, I felt something in me split; a part of me stepping into the role of guardian. The one who would guide the rest of me through. The witness, not the experiencer. My inner voice instructed me:

*Don't hold him too tightly. Don't ask why the blanket is draped like that. Don't move too fast in case the table shifts. Don't do **anything** that might make you confront the clinical reality.*

Then I searched for what was the same. His nose, just like Bubbie's. The freckle on the side of his temple. The roundness of his fingernails. The way his ankles rolled slightly outward. The small blue tattoo dots at the center of his throat and collarbone, radiation markers from when he was seventeen.

I turned to look around the room.

Aunt Rosemary was crying quietly, holding a glossy white page I assumed was her letter to Gabe. April sat beside her. My mom was stroking his head, tears falling as she called him her darling boy. Sean wept and walked slow circles around the room. James kept whispering:

"I can't believe this is happening."

When I'd imagined losses like this before—my dad's, especially —I always pictured myself collapsing into hysterics: screaming, throwing up, being carried out. But when the time actually came, it always resolved the same way. I could stay in the room.

Here it was again.

And when I looked around, I saw that everyone else could too.

This was what it meant to be alive and to love someone who no longer was. This was the experience of being human.

After we all settled in, it was time to begin.

In my meditation the day before, I had received guidance from Gabe's spirit and my own intuition about how to proceed. I opened the bag I was carrying and first took out a bottle of essential oil called *Breathe Deep* from his room—a sharp-smelling blend of cardamom, peppermint, and eucalyptus. I anointed his head, the space between his eyebrows, his chest, and his hands.

Next, I took out some of the crystals from his apartment: smoky quartz, green calcite, and a few others. I gently placed them on his torso. Over his heart, I laid our grandfather Werner's silver medallion from the army. It was something Art had sent over from his own collection of treasured belongings.

We stood in a quiet circle around my peaceful-looking brother.

I opened my bag again and pulled out a stack of papers. They were letters to Gabe from some of his loved ones and mentors. I had received clear instructions from his spirit on who to reach out to, and I'd texted each person, inviting them

to write whatever they wished to send with him before cremation. Like all memorials, I knew this was as much for the
living—for our healing and closure—as it might be for his
soul.

I read them aloud, facing him. Halfway through the second
letter, I paused and asked myself: *Why am I reading these directly to
him?* But it felt right to look at his face while I shared these final
messages of love and gratitude.

After that, each of us read our own letter aloud.

When it was my turn as the last letter to be shared, I took off
my shoes and walked barefoot around the room, clutching the
thick paper I'd written on. I began:

"Gabe, our connection is beyond words, beyond bodies, beyond-
beyond-beyond. I can't believe I got to be the one who was like
your twin, your ally, and your companion through so many life
journeys.

There are so many people who would have wanted that role.
And now I have to fully grow into the person I must be for it to
have been mine. The version of me that *you* always saw and
reflected back, even when I couldn't."

I thought about the day I cried next to him on the balcony.

*You've never been the problem, Al. You'll always be the solution to your
own life.*

I looked down at my letter and cleared my throat.

"I will learn to do that for myself now. I love you. I feel you with
me, and I see the ways we will still be able to work together here
on Earth."

I glanced up and saw my family and friends listening, some

wiping away tears. It felt vulnerable, this spiritual way of speaking. Would they find it too flowery? Too abstract?

But in that moment, I saw that they understood.

I continued.

"Thank you for being who you are. It's making this flow easier, with more love than I thought possible. Thank you for protecting me with your unending patience, love, and humor."

I thought again of our final visit: the way he had let me feel safe in my sorrow, the movie nights, the laughter, the shorthand of our private sibling language. A continuation of how it had always been since childhood.

"Our relationship is the epitome of good fortune. I don't know if anyone has ever been as lucky. Somehow, I forgot that. And now I remember."

My heart bloomed with the truth: how lucky I was to have Gabe as my brother. Over the years, so many people had commented on the bond we shared as something rare, something they hadn't seen before. Gabe was my protector, my mentor, and my closest friend for thirty-five *years*. And I would carry our journey forward into whatever came next.

For a moment, the months I had spent feeling sorry for myself dissolved in the face of love and gratitude. I could see what the years of our sibling relationship had been preparing me for. I would have to get bigger than the unfairness of it all. Bigger than the physical and emotional pain. I would have to anchor myself in the infinite and spiritual truth of what we had shared.

"Anything you need done on Earth, I will commit to for as long as I'm here. When there's a choice to be generous, I'll choose it, just like you always did. I will treat my body and soul with reverence. I will care for our family, and let your love and wisdom move through me."

As I said those words, I felt the weight of responsibility—how much would still be asked of me—but I could also feel my strength. I could do it.

"I won't sweat the small stuff," I promised. I looked at his still, strong body. "Brother and sister in every dimension and in all universes."

I thought of all the mystics and healers who told us we'd been twins across many lifetimes; who even could map it out through our astrology charts, Human Design and numerology. I knew it was true. When it came to my connection with my brother, under all other emotions was a peaceful contentment that ran deeper than this life. But now, in this lifetime, that contentment had come to an end.

"Gabe, I love you so much."

I finished my letter with a tearful exhale and laid it gently on his chest with the others.

It was nearly the end of our allotted time. The energy in the room began to shift, crackling with the unspoken awareness that it was time to complete. I could sense it in our postures, in the way we moved, each of us slowly reaching the threshold of what we could hold.

Once we walked out that door, it would be over. We would never see him again. The sensation was paralyzing—*needing* to leave, while hating the idea of it.

When we opened that door, we would walk back through the portal, and into the world where we could only see Gabe in our pictures, memories, and dreams.

I noticed Aunt Rosemary gesturing to the guys, holding up that same white paper I had seen earlier. It turned out to be the lunch menu from her country club. In her urgency to nurture, she had brought it so we'd know we could order lunch afterward.

"They do a great lobster roll," she said.

Another surreal, funny moment; something Gabe and I would have cracked up about. Both sides of our Italian and Jewish family always prepared to feed people in any circumstance, even this one.

Eventually, each person in the room made their final pass, brushing fingertips over Gabe's shoulder or hand, then continuing out the door.

Mom paused in front of him, touching his shirt.

"I always loved this one on him," she said, wiping her eyes.

She looked so small and vulnerable in her sundress and platform sandals. I watched as she leaned down and gently kissed her son goodbye and was awed by her bravery.

Mom told me to take whatever final time I needed before she left. And suddenly, it was just the two of us.

I gazed down at my brother one last time. The right words had been spoken. The precious objects were in place. Soon, it would all become sacred ash. There was nothing else to do. Part of me longed for one more ritual, one more prayer, some *other* final act. But my system was tapped. And truthfully, I knew we were complete.

I leaned down, pressed my warm forehead to his cold one, and closed my eyes.

I don't want to leave you. But it's time.

I stood and walked toward the door, astonished with each step that we were all somehow able to surrender to the permanence of never seeing him again.

As I closed the door and stepped back into the hallway, I realized I had accessed a new understanding of the human experience.

Now I was certain. We have something inside us beyond personality, and it's designed to walk forward, even when we aren't prepared for the loss. Even when we believed we never could be.

I thought of all the people across time who had been forced to say goodbye without warning: watching their beloved disappear to the sea, left on a snowy mountain, buried along a dusty road. Unceremoniously separated in war camps, or losing each other on a chaotic battlefield. Walking away from a makeshift grave of rubble, given far less space for reverence than I was afforded now.

This mysterious thing inside allows us to go on; for self-preservation, for the continuation of the story. Even when we know we'll yearn for their voice and company for the rest of our days.

Back in the car, I leaned my head against the window. We drove past grim-looking faded storefronts, the sky heavy with dull gray clouds as we rejoined the highway. The view outside matched the way I felt.

There were many more decisions to make. A long list of tasks still ahead. But for now, I closed my eyes and let myself begin to digest what had taken place. Each hour of the day held its own necessary trauma, especially the last few.

Would these days leave permanent scars?

I didn't know.

But this was the path laid before me now.

And my job was to walk it.

APRIL, 2019: MIAMI BEACH, FL

THE NAP SHIRT

I turned over again in the hotel bed across from Anne, trying to shake the panic fluttering through my body and finally drift off. The room was dark and quiet except for the soft buzz of the air-conditioning. Everyone had meant well by having me stay at the hotel instead of Gabe's, but I couldn't sleep here.

So far, the only place I'd been able to find rest was in his bed, wearing sweats from his closet. The only food I could stand to eat were the shelf-stable groceries we'd bought together when he first moved in.

Yesterday morning was the first time I'd been able to prepare something for myself. I staggered into the kitchen and weakly poured some cornflakes and raisins into a small bowl, splashing almond milk on top.

My vision flickered in and out of focus before finally settling on the bowl. Somehow, this bowl of cereal felt like more effort than anything else I'd done yet. I exhaled and steadied myself. A small sense of accomplishment bloomed as I raised the spoon to my mouth.

Wow, I thought. *This is what it feels like to attempt a normal, adrenaline-free task when you're this devastated.*

It was all temporary. Tomorrow we'd throw out the Tupperware of leftovers then do the laundry and wash the sheets; letting go of the last places Gabe's human form had touched. Someone had eventually picked up the pajama bottoms from over his slippers. When it happened, James and I both winced at the same time, even through we knew his apartment couldn't stay frozen in time. I was glad I would still have the box of cereal for a little while longer.

The days following the cremation ceremony were a blur of horrible but necessary logistics: planning, decisions, phone calls. In the midst of it all, there were also beautifully moving virtual memorials with his business and Qigong communities.

Anne, Maskell, and a few other core members of the Evo-Med team had flown in to be present, staying at a nearby hotel, and we'd shared a special dinner to honor Gabe and all of their collective work together, along with other meetings.

But now I was really exhausted. I needed space from everyone. I'd also been trying to reach my doctors back in L.A. Should I really be taking these antidepressants? Could anyone even adjust to them while adding in some PTSD? No one had called me back yet.

That evening, I had gone to dinner at Puerto Sagua with Anne, Mom, and our family friend Celeste. Without thinking, I ordered what Gabe and I always got. When the steaming plate of roast chicken, white rice, black beans, and plantains was placed in front of me, I burst into tears. Through gasps and heaving sobs, I managed to explain:

"The last time I was here was with Gabe...and this is what we had. I'm sorry. I'm not ready to be here. I can't do this yet."

I put my head in my hands and cried into the plate. After a moment, I slipped away to the tiny bathroom in the back of the restaurant. The floor was littered with damp tissue paper. The neon pink soap dispenser was nearly empty after being used up by the day's beachgoers.

I shut myself into a narrow stall and sobbed.

When Dad died, I learned to cry silently so I wouldn't scare my college housemates, especially the girl I was sharing a room with at the time. We had been close, but our friendship was shaken by this big change, just as she was getting more serious with her older boyfriend. I remembered my first night back at school in that little Boston bedroom, with both of them there. He was in his twenties; uncomfortably clingy and oddly content to be crammed into a two-bedroom apartment with the four of us. From the bed across the room, he looked up at me that first night.

"Hey," he said awkwardly. "I heard about your dad."

That was it. Nothing else.

"Yeah," I replied weakly, sliding under my blankets and putting on my Discman headphones so I wouldn't have to hear them anymore. Although she wasn't my roommate for long after that, that was when the practice of soundless weeping began.

Years of pretending with everyone my age followed. I never fully broke down. I was too afraid to lose control when it felt like my life was just beginning.

But this next loss came after years of being out of practice with that toxic ability to repress sorrow.

As I sat in the stall, a friend texted me:

> Thinking of you <3 How are you today?

I replied:

> At the moment I'm crying in the bathroom at our favorite restaurant in Miami. But I'm gonna be okay. It was just too soon to be here.

This level of grief, I was learning, was like that. Something could be fine—and then, in a split second, it absolutely was *not*. My job was to keep meeting myself in the moment, and to course-correct as needed.

I wished the current version of me could time-travel to 2004, burst into that bedroom in Boston, kick the weird boyfriend out, and give my younger self the space to be openly sad on her first night back. I hadn't been able to do that then, but I could take care of myself now. And maybe that could heal her backwards in time.

When I returned to the table, my meal was boxed up. The check had been paid, and everyone was ready to go.

I was grateful.

Celeste handed me a blue paper bag with a sad smile.

"Honey, I got this for you when your mom and I were shopping."

It was from The Gap right across the street, where I'd spent so many summers buying back-to-school clothes growing up. Sweaters and jeans were always on sale in the sweltering August heat of Miami, but they'd be perfect a few weeks later back in Long Island. I opened the bag and found a navy cotton long-sleeved shirt. The word "NAP" was stitched in white college lettering across the front.

"Thanks, Celeste," I said. "At least someone approves of me wanting to sleep all the time."

After dinner, we headed back to the hotel. The plan was for Mom and Celeste to share one room, while I stayed with Anne in another. For the first few hours, it was comforting, like a sleep-over. We texted and connected with other people in our inner circle who were moving through this strange, awful experience alongside us while chatting on fluffy white beds.

Anne and I had been friends for years by then. When Anne decided she loved you, it was with the devotion of a sister: fierce, protective, and attuned to your needs. From the moment she arrived in Miami with the team, she'd been watching over me carefully, even though she herself was reeling from the loss of her closest work confidante and ally.

We had met over a decade earlier when we worked together in admissions at an acupuncture school and became fast friends. We left our jobs the same week—me to return full-time to my own healing practice, and Anne to join Gabe and Maskell in launching their company. She had planned to work with Gabe for the rest of her career.

Around midnight, we turned off the lights and tried to sleep. I watched Anne's glossy black hair spill over the pillow, listened to her breathing, and thought about what a long, hard day it had been for her. I wanted to fall asleep so she could finally rest.

But no matter how I turned, I couldn't.

I felt like an iPhone trying to plug into an Android charger. I wasn't able to sleep anywhere else at night—not yet.

Around 3 a.m., I tiptoed out of bed and quietly gathered my bag and keys in the dark.

"I can tell you can't fall asleep," Anne said sleepily, as if her nervous system was tuned into mine.

"Sorry," I whispered. "It's not that I don't want to share a room with you, or that I'm not glad you're here. I just...I can't sleep anywhere else yet."

She lifted her head and blinked as I turned on my phone's flashlight.

"No, I totally get it. Go be where you need to be. I'll see you tomorrow."

I took the elevator down to the silent lobby and called an Uber. As soon as I got in, I exhaled and found my shoulders dropping and the knot in my back loosening.

Relief.

The car dropped me off at Gabe's building. I took the elevator upstairs. The moon shimmered over the bay, the sky still the darkest blue. When I opened the door, I felt myself further unwind.

His couch. His coffee table. His cereal still on the counter.

Safety.

I reached to turn on a lamp. The bulb blinked a few times before finally lighting the room. Then, as I walked past his laptop, it powered on.

A Google search flickered onto the screen. I froze and stepped closer.

It was a search for Venice Beach—where I currently lived.

I had used his laptop throughout the week to handle his bills and paperwork, but I hadn't seen this search before. And now here it was, glowing on the screen: images of the bike lane I rode each day, the candy-colored cottages along the canals, the rainbow-painted lifeguard stand, the skate park.

The screen scrolled on its own, as if someone were browsing. My heart pounded. I felt it; the unmistakable sensation that I was not alone.

Gabe was here.

His presence was so strong I felt nearly frozen in place, stunned by the weight of it. Then I heard it—not aloud, but within me:

I'm here. It's okay. Go to my room.

I had felt this kind of guidance before; when my body was gently led into postures during energetic or spiritual channeling. I moved toward his room.

I was drawn to the back of his closet.

There, I saw an open mailer envelope I hadn't noticed before—not even when James, Sean, and I had chosen his final outfit. It was addressed to my house in Venice.

Inside, something soft was rolled up.I pulled it out and unwrapped it. It was the exact *NAP* shirt Celeste had given me at dinner.

Gabe had planned to send me the same one, knowing I had been so tired lately. I held it close. This was his way of saying, *Rest is allowed.*

My brother was everywhere and nowhere, all at once.

I was blown away by his spiritual ability to connect with the physical world. But more than anything, I missed him being here in the physical, too.

I dropped to my knees and cried.

Everything I had been holding in since arriving in Miami finally poured out. It was the first moment I'd been truly alone since it happened, free to let it move through me. I worried about waking his neighbors, but once it began I couldn't stop; the grief worked its way through until there was nothing left.

I could feel Gabe there, bearing witness.

Eventually, I stood up, dazed from crying but with the agony washed away for now. I walked back into the living room and opened the front door. Birds were beginning to chirp. Car engines hummed in the distance. The sky had shifted into soft streaks of blue and orange.

The sun would rise soon.

I closed the door and walked back through the apartment. I took off my damp pajamas, pulled the *NAP* shirt over my head, and crawled into bed.

Finally, I could sleep.

JUNE, 2019: MIAMI BEACH, FL

THE MAD QUEEN

That summer, a memory kept rising up in my mind.

Two days before I flew out from L.A. to visit Gabe for the last time, I had gone to a concert at a small venue on the east side of town. The artist was one of my favorites, a singer-song-writer with a melodic R&B flavor named Rhye.

Although I had planned to go with a few friends, a stomach bug had swept through the group the day of the show. Everyone else canceled, but I stuck with the plan.

I remembered it with complete clarity. Standing at the bar, watching tiny bubbles rise slowly in my glass of champagne. A petite dark-haired woman in a trendy denim jumper caught my eye. Something shifted in her gaze, and then she walked over.

"Hi," she said, her voice tinged with hesitation. "So... this is going to sound strange. It's never happened to me before, but I just got this *message* in my head and I feel like I'm supposed to tell you?"

Her eyes scanned my face, checking to see if I was open, so I responded with a friendly smile.

It had just turned midnight, officially my birthday. As I

approached the bar, I had quietly asked Spirit to send me something about turning 35. *Make it positive, please.* Seconds later, this woman appeared with a mysterious message. I was more than intrigued.

She took a breath. "Something is going to take you out of L.A. this year. You're going to have to leave, but it'll be the right thing to do."

I laughed and set down my glass. "Well, you're already right. Last week I had to move out of my apartment because of *mold*. And it officially became my birthday about three minutes ago, so I guess you're giving me the first forecast of my year."

She widened her eyes and smiled at the synchronicity.

"Wow. Well, if you *do* leave L.A. for real, I hope it's for something good." She lifted her glass to mine. We clinked. Then she walked away.

Back in the present moment, I realized she'd been right. I had left L.A. and yes, it was the right thing to do.

But it wasn't for something good.

It was becoming clear: My once-beautiful time in California was done. Not on pause. Not waiting for me.

I could stop trying to save that life, because it was over.

That thought made me sad and disappointed, but more than anything, I was numb. It had been six weeks since Gabe died, and I could barely move. I'd already been exhausted before the tragedy, but now I found myself crawling into bed every afternoon for a long nap like a baby.

Later I'd learn this wasn't dysfunction—it was a neurologically and physiologically valid response to both grief and mold exposure. But all I knew then was that sleep was the only place I could process what my waking body couldn't bear. When I was asleep, I could finally digest the horror. Even though it meant waking up to those first awful seconds where I had to remember he was gone all over again.

And yet, it just made everyone worry more.

Because my mental health had already started to become fragile before Gabe died, people assumed my staying in bed meant a deeper spiral: depression, disassociation, *danger*. Mom and others tried to lure me downstairs to sit in the sun by the pool or walk to the Whole Foods across the street to find something I might want to eat.

I knew my mother meant well; she thrives on company. In her view, the way to recover was to be around others. But walking under the garish supermarket lights, steering my cart around shoppers debating kombucha flavors, felt like wandering through a nightmare.

Down at the pool, people sipped cocktails and bumped house music as the sun slipped over the bay, casting a honeyed glow over the water and sky. Every interaction, even just a friendly nod, felt like a nail I had to crawl over.

It was *so* not where I needed to be.

The reality was settling in: the part of my life where Gabe existed was truly over. It was like the moment in a movie when a beloved character dies and you realize the film is winding down. It made me feel ancient and like the best years of my life were way behind me.

I couldn't believe *Gabe*, of all people, hadn't been given more time. I was devastated and furious, and well-meaning but clueless people said things like:

"Don't worry. One day, you'll smile again,"

or:

"After this, you'll move on and have a happy life."

Hearing those words made me feel sick. I didn't *want* to move on. The very suggestion felt repugnant. I couldn't stomach the idea that he would become insignificant, or just another loss I'd learn to live with.

However that didn't meant I wanted to *take* my life. I had brushed close enough to that feeling just a few weeks before, but I definitely wasn't there now. This was something else: a level of devastation and grief where I didn't care what happened next, because nothing could reverse the only thing I cared about.

Gabe's apartment was on the 11th floor. Someone considered an "expert" told my mom I shouldn't be left alone in a high-rise with a balcony. They insisted that my own opinion on my mental health shouldn't be trusted for at least five years—even if I *seemed* better.

A kind of vigil began as soon as I arrived in Miami. Even after Mom realized I wasn't in that level of crisis, I still wasn't allowed to be alone in the apartment or on the balcony, where Gabe and I had so recently watched manatees swim and laughed over tea in our matching mugs. Sneaking back that night from the hotel had been the only exception.

The night before Gabe died, the final season of *Game of Thrones* had premiered. It had sparked the Easter Sunday "last supper" gathering at my place in Venice. In the weeks after his passing, the show became a strange lifeline for his closest friends and me.

We created a group chat called **THE FAMILY** and live-texted through each episode—sharing jokes, reactions, and commentary. It gave us one small thing to look forward to each week, even if just for an hour.

When I messaged about the awful logistics I was handling, or the unbearable anger that kept erupting, James would reply in the chat with GIFs of Daenerys Targaryen commanding her dragons with a sharp

"DRACARYS!"

Halfway through the season, Daenerys lost everyone she loved and descended into grief-induced insanity. She became "The Mad Queen," the final villain of the series.

It was then that I understood her even more.

It felt like I was seen as fragile enough to break, yet still able to lead in the wake of this shocking loss. I was no longer the free-spirited baby of the family, but an adult only child suddenly at the helm of the next moves.

I was making decisions about Gabe's personal effects: organizing his estate, navigating serious professional conversations, and witnessing the painful unraveling of the projects he had poured himself into. I tracked down bank accounts and searched for passwords to his phone and laptop, trying to retrieve what was needed while still honoring his privacy.

I was trusted with major responsibilities, yet the sleep and solitude I needed to recover were misinterpreted, as if my withdrawal signaled a risk rather than a form of survival.

I was also beginning to feel increasingly anxious and irritable about still being in Gabe's apartment. The longer he was gone, the less comfortable it felt. The staff and tenants looked at me with pity, or that's at least what I felt.

And the gym. The gym had become its own form of haunting.

It had a glass door and a clear view of the first of three treadmills—the one Gabe had been walking on when he collapsed. I found myself looping around the building to avoid passing it on the way to the elevator or the door outside.

One night I decided I couldn't keep living with that spike of dread every time I left the apartment. Maybe exposure therapy was the only way through.

I pulled on leggings, a sports bra, and a tank top. I laced up my sneakers. My heart was pounding in my ears as I walked into the empty room.

I stepped onto the treadmill.

"Hey," I said out loud to the screen with its buttons that suddenly looked a bit like a face. "You're not allowed to fuck with me anymore. This ends now."

I turned it on, and the tread belt started slowly at first. I cranked it up until I was jogging, sweat beading on my skin, breath loud in my chest. After a few minutes, I slowed it down to a brisk walk, my arms swinging like the power-walkers I remembered from the mall as a kid.

Eventually, I stepped off. I pushed open the door and rode the elevator back up. I never became a frequent visitor of the building's gym, but after that night, I could walk past the glass without looking away.

In the second month of living in Gabe's building, far from my friends, the loneliness sharpened. I thought maybe it would help to connect with someone who didn't know me or the story of what had happened. Someone I could pretend with.

One afternoon, a young couple started chatting with me at the pool on a day I'd felt okay enough to float in the water on my own. They had the pale skin and four-pack of craft beer that came with moving to Florida from Vermont. I was tilted back in a lounge chair, face up to the sun, savoring a break from everyone and the endless list of decisions.

They had just moved in that day and were eager to meet a fellow resident. Suddenly, I wanted to try on the costume of a non-grieving person. They reminded me of the kind of people I'd joke around with at a backyard BBQ. I let the social version of me out—the friendly, can-talk-to-anyone girl—and accepted the offer of a beer.

Why was I visiting? Oh, a relative of mine had just moved in, I said casually. And for just a moment, I let myself dip into that small, imagined reality. I could remember when this was still true; when that had been the reason why I was here at the pool. Maybe I could spend the afternoon in easy conversation, and not have to break the ice with tragedy.

Maybe two strangers could just see me as a fun person in their cool new building, and not the Mad Queen of Grief.

We chatted for about thirty minutes. It was light and pleasant. I gave them some suggestions for good dinner spots, we exchanged numbers and even made a loose plan for later in the week. It felt like a breath of normalcy, to access an echo of the me I used to be.

That evening, while Mom and I were outside Gabe's apartment watering plants and going over logistics for the upcoming move-out, the couple walked by again.

"Oh, *hi!*" the wife said brightly. "Turns out we are *literally* your new neighbors!"

I froze. They were moving into the unit next door—what used to be Henry's place. I introduced them to Mom, and within a minute, the conversation turned to the relative we were "visiting."

"Maybe we'll get to meet him," the husband offered warmly.

Before I could intervene or explain, Mom turned toward them and gently said,

"Actually, it was my son who lived here, and sadly, he passed away."

Their smiles dropped instantly, replaced by a look of unease.

My cheeks flushed.

The one time Mom decided not to be private about her grief. The one time I didn't lead with the heartbreak—and now I looked like a total freaking weirdo. It was almost comedic. I imagined I seemed like a kid they met at a hotel pool who'd made up some elaborate story, and now they were meeting her parents in line at the breakfast buffet.

Sorry, we hope she hasn't been bothering you too much while you're on vacation!

"Oh, I—we're so sorry, we had no idea," stammered the husband, as his wife chimed in, "Yes, so sorry... of course."

The couple turned away, avoiding eye contact with me, and hurried into their new apartment. They had clearly decided not to talk to The Mad Queen again.

But then a glimmer of light: Dylan came to visit.

He had been one of my college housemates and a lasting friend since we first met freshman year in the Northeastern cafeteria. I remembered feeling a spark in the air that day, a sense we'd stay connected. And we had.

Dylan knew how to have fun *and* how to organize it: throwing a picnic basket into the Jeep, booking the ferry to Sausalito, hiding a secret joint in the glove compartment for just the right moment.

Back in college, his talent for elevating a plan met the creativity and wide network of our little crew, and combined, it all created a kind of alchemy. Our small apartment became the backdrop for unforgettable nights, our parties legendary among our friends. That brightness wove joy into my college years, even with the heaviness at home.

There was our twenty-first birthday "Pink Party," when we turned *everything pink*—the walls, outfits, accessories, somehow even the beer. And the massive toga party we hosted during a historic heat wave, with Patrick, our fashion-savvy roommate and resident DJ, designing togas in every fabric from gold chainlink to neon flower to paisley. We hauled a huge ice luge up to the roof, perfect for the 100-degree weather. Even Gabe came up for that one.

With Dylan, I always felt a little braver. In that way, he reminded me of my brother. Midway through freshman year, he encouraged us to buy bicycles. I was nervous; riding in the city felt daunting. I hadn't been on a bike since looping slowly around the block in fifth grade. But we got them. Our other roomie Becky, always cheerful and supportive, instigated our "early morning bike rides," pulling me out in our PJs to circle the neighborhood as we built up our confidence.

As we adjusted to busier city streets, Dylan led the brigade at first. But soon we were all confidently riding through Boston; along the Charles River, through Chinatown, trekking up Mission Hill and flying down with glee, navigating cobblestones on the way to part-time jobs on Newbury Street. Dylan even added a woven basket to the front of his bike, so my mini-dachshund Chas could come along. The reconnection to bicycles has been an enduring gift. I still ride to this day.

It was early June when Dylan walked into the Miami apartment, fresh from his Boston flight wearing a crisp checkered button-down, khaki shorts, and well-worn leather flip-flops. His once-shaggy blonde hair was now neatly coiffed. Mom and I had avocado toast and mimosas waiting, realizing at the same time how much we'd needed a guest who felt both fresh and familiar — and how glad we were that it was him.

That afternoon, he came with us to the Hidden Arches, sat with Marco Polo in his lap, and talked real estate with Aunt Rosemary. After dinner out, we dropped Mom back at the house, then headed to the apartment. It was sad and surreal hosting Dylan in what had been Gabe's space, but I was still grateful. The nutrient of friendship was worth the weirdness.

When we got back, we changed into swimsuits and went downstairs to the hot tub, the city skyline glittering above.

"It's pretty crazy, right?" I said, watching him through the steam. "I haven't had people who *know me*-know me here since the first week. And I don't think anyone realizes, like…"

"Oh yeah," Dylan said quickly. "I mean, this is a lot, all of it. It's so much."

"I hope it's not too much to be around," I said, my throat tightening.

I thought of the times I had needed friends but been too scared to ask, or of the people who disappeared until the crisis passed.

"No. It's a lot, but not too much," he said, pouring Prosecco into one of the pink flamingo pool cups Mom had bought when Gabe moved in. He looked up, serious now.

"Listen. When your dad died, we were kids. We didn't handle it well at the apartment. Nobody knew what to do at first, and—"

"And I didn't know how to *ask!*" I blurted, remembering how I cried into a pillow instead of saying what I needed.

"Well, I'm an adult now," Dylan said. "And this time, I *do* know what to do. I can show up the right way. And I will."

His words landed with a tenderness so sharp it almost hurt.

That weekend, we floated in the ocean as storm clouds rolled in, got massages, and ate at Puerto Sagua without crying. One

night on the balcony, we did a fire ritual—writing down everything stirring up chaos, including one particularly infuriating
person involved in closing out Gabe's business, to burn away.

I dropped the papers into a bowl, and Dylan lit the utility
lighter with the same flourish he'd once used in his crème brûlée
phase in college. The fire flared so high we shrieked and rushed it
outside, Dylan dousing it with water in a frenzy before laughing at
the soggy ashes. I felt sure we'd cleared some of the bad energy,
even if we almost burned the place down in the process.

I didn't have to pretend to be someone else, and I didn't have to
explain. My old friend knew my life before, during, and after.
Dylan wasn't there to act as a therapist, but he also wasn't afraid of
my grief, and he didn't try to avoid the story.

This was the chapter I was in, but I was still *me*. I couldn't have
imagined how badly I would need someone to just show up and
know how to do this.

As a woman in my thirties and not a college kid like when Dad
died, I had assumed it would be easier to ask for support. But it
wasn't. In some ways, it was harder. My friends were busy: full
lives, big careers, little kids, new homes. Some had calendars
booked a year in advance. Who had the time to step into this? It
turned out it had to be someone willing to *make* the time.

I was learning that prior connection, or even professional
expertise, doesn't guarantee someone will know what to do
around grief—or that they'll have the capacity to follow through.

But in that moment, my friend did. And I received the medicine of having someone stay, witness, and treat me as whole, even
in the midst of breaking apart.

JUNE, 2019: LOS ANGELES, CA

THE PERFECT BIKE

I laid back in my seat on the plane and closed my eyes.
It was done.

Last week, I had flown from Miami to LAX to officially shut down my life in Venice. I boxed up what I could, shipped it to Mom's house in Long Island, and got rid of everything else—including my favorite and first purchase after arriving: a pink beach-cruiser bicycle.

That bike had been my main source of transportation for the last three years in California. I still smiled when remembering the adventure of buying it.

A few days after I had first arrived in Venice in Fall of 2016, I sat at the local coffee shop. It was a two-story wooden cabin just a few houses from the beach, called The Cow's End. It had red-framed windows and an enormous fake cow hanging off the roof.

I ordered their signature drink, *The Latte Latino*. It was espresso poured into steamed half and half and condensed milk; rich and cozy, with the scent of cinnamon. I sat in the October sunshine on a white plastic chair in front of the café, letting the pleasure of it all wash over me with the ocean breeze.

This is my life now.

That day, I had just crunched the numbers for my business. With a few months still to go, I was already at my highest profit margin ever. It had been an awesome year—my practice was booked out and I was having so much fun creating different programs with clients from around the world.

The scaling process wasn't perfect: I was always "on," reaching for the next goal, taking clients in every and any time zone, then jumping on calls with my coaches to keep the momentum alive. My social life in Chicago dimmed under the weight of that schedule, and my relationship with my boyfriend eventually faded too, overshadowed by the intensity of my focus on career and practice. I hadn't yet learned how to hold both.

Of course, building a home and sustaining a relationship is its own kind of spiritual practice. But for many years it felt like a conflict; I could pour into love, or I could pour into my purpose. In my romantic life, the fire for my unconventional work was intriguing at first, and eventually became one of the issues.

There was always something or someone to give my energy to in the business. After years of building toward success, I had lost sight of where I ended and the work began. I kept telling myself the next big push would finally feel like self-care.

The week before I came to find my place in Venice, I'd Airbnb'd what ended up being a glorified tent in someone's backyard, traffic buzzing just beyond the fence. I was on deadline for a tele-summit, so I just went with it, writing and recording an entire digital program from the tent—before flying to New York for Bubbie's birthday.

Why *didn't* a nice hotel feel like a non-negotiable? What would it have felt like to celebrate my new home lying in crisp white sheets, recording peacefully from a quiet room with sunlight filtering through the blinds?

Gabe often pointed out that I would spend thousands on coaching or courses, but couldn't manage to take my vitamins consistently. He had a point. After so many years of feeling responsible for others' wellbeing, I'd developed a blind spot about my own.

There was a thread of self-sacrifice woven through some of these bigger choices, as if I were waiting for the day when my comfort could matter as much as my mission—or when it *could* be the mission.

But with this move from Chicago to L.A., I'd vowed to start a new era. One where I could have abundance personally *and* professionally, where I wouldn't trade one for the other.

When I added up the numbers, I called Gabe.

A tear slid down my cheek as I told him the total.

I had been scrappy throughout my twenties—often working a second job along with my practice—always waiting for the epic moment I had been promised since my first personal growth training in college. But here in my 30s it was different. Finally.

"I mean, you did it, Al. It's *incredible*," Gabe said.

Then he paused.

"I think it's important to stop and feel this. Honor the milestone."

At the time, I didn't yet have neighborhood friends in Venice, and I wasn't sure who else to share it with. So I closed my laptop, walked to the beach, and headed to The Cow's End. I was determined to order the most decadent coffee on the menu.

As I sat enjoying my drink, I started talking to the man next to me. He was leaning back, tanned legs and sandy bare feet stretched out, with wavy sun-bleached hair still streaked with saltwater—the signature look of so many Venice locals. Soon, I would have it too.

In front of him was a bicycle that could only be described as fabulous. It was electric blue with wide handlebars, out of which rainbow streamers danced. Tiny glowing lights wrapped the frame and wheels, like lightning bugs in motion.

I grinned. "Okay, you know what I'm going to ask."

He looked at his ride, then back at me, laughing.

"You need a bike? There's only one man to visit in Venice. The Bicycle Whisperer will hook you *up*."

Thirty minutes later, a cab dropped me off in an alley.

I checked the address saved in my phone and walked slowly down the street, passing cute craftsman houses and rows of recycling bins, wondering if this the right spot.

That's when I looked up and saw a big blue sign hanging off a post and flapping in the wind, printed with the words **BICYCLE WHISPERER.**

Then I turned and saw him: The Whisperer himself. In front of a garage overflowing with wheels and tubes, he was mid–tune-up, wearing a pristine white tee and navy Chuck Taylors.

His name, I later learned, was Lance, born and raised in Venice. He had the look of a true local, the kind that were more about wheels than a surfboard. I mentioned I had just moved to town and needed a new bike.

His smile widened. "Your first Venice Beach bicycle! Wow. We gotta do at least a *touch* of a cruiser. But for you, let's see... I'm thinking hybrid."

Lance moved toward a sea of bikes in every color and paused in front of one, considering. Then he rolled it out: a pastel pink cruiser with a brown leather seat and matching handlebars. A large woven basket was fastened to the front.On the frame, written in shimmering silver cursive:

Nadine.

"That's the one!" I laughed. "You knew it."

He polished her up, checked the tires, then clipped the sale tag from the handlebar. The bike had playful style, but all the quality features for a reliable, comfortable ride. It was perfect.

"Now, Nadine's not a name you'd *think* to pick for your bike," Lance said, "but suddenly it's there and you're like—oh, *hells* yeah!"

Soon I was pedaling toward the beach, heading up the wide

slope at the end of Rose Avenue where the world-famous Venice Beach boardwalk begins.

At the top of the hill, the view exploded in every direction:

The endless stretch of warm sand before the Pacific. Massive mountains to the right, looking almost hand-painted in the distance. To the left, the winding boardwalk with its beach bars and pop-up shops, alive with legendary locals—like Harry Perry, Venice's most famous rollerblading guitarist. Around him, other musicians played, fortune tellers beckoned, and a juggler balanced his act beneath a talkative parrot perched on his head. Further down, the voice of the Freak Show barker drew people in to see two-headed turtles and a sword swallower.

The paved bike path curved through the sand toward the Fishing Pier and the surfers beyond. At the very end of the trail was 29th Avenue, and the location of my new apartment.

The day I got Nadine was the day I felt it: I'd really made it to the next chapter. Venice Beach had welcomed me with the most beautiful view and the perfect new ride.

It was the beginning of almost three years of incredible adventure. And now, it was over.

In my final hour before leaving for my flight out of L.A. for good, I looked out onto the terrace and realized I still hadn't figured out what to do with Nadine.

The few short days back in Venice had been a blur of packing, mailing, and cleaning while coughing through a bad cold that hit the second I stepped into my apartment. My body screamed for rest, but the timeline didn't allow for it.

I was foggy from the whirlwind when I saw her—a girl walking down my block on her way to the beach. I had an idea.

"Hey," I called out weakly. "Would you want this bicycle? I need to leave for the airport, like, right now."

The blonde woman in a tie-dyed sundress and flip-flops stopped. She peered into the basket, then slowly circled the bike.

"Hmmm," she said. "You know what? I still don't have my bike for Burning Man! I can ride this baby into the ground on the playa and then toss it or scrap it or whatever."

My shoulders dropped.

That's exactly how I feel.

Ridden into the ground.

And now everything is scrapped.

"Thanks!" she called out brightly, wheeling Nadine away.

I pictured my pink bike riding out to her swan song, joining thousands of West Coast tech executives in tiny metallic shorts and desert goggles. I could see it now: Nadine glowing with fairy lights, leaning against an art car, surrounded by rainbow braids and dusty faces in ecstasy, weaving through bodies dancing in furry boots. *There are worse ways to go.*

It was the dramatic end to one of my most exciting eras. I had left behind my comfortable, established life in Chicago—a city I loved and felt at home in—to try something new and expansive. When it was on, it was *electric*. Prosperity flowed and creativity sparked. The early months carried the growing pains of leaving behind the comfort of a relationship and longtime friends, but I still had a few old pals and family close, and soon opened to the thrill of new possibilities.

Venice was home to various entrepreneurial networks *and* a teaching community centered on desire and intimacy. In that environment, I allowed myself to become more vulnerable and present. I found friendships and romances that fully reignited my personal life—messy and exciting in equal measure.

It was a wonderful time and place to have a healing practice. Clients came to the West Coast for intimate group retreats, where I brought in local chefs and practitioners to help create profound shared experiences. That inspiration fueled new offerings, along with daily livestreams recorded right from the beach, so the energy could be shared as it unfolded.

Outside of work, life was a full-on West Coast immersion, so quintessentially L.A. it was almost funny. Mornings often started with a ride down the beach to the famous 9 a.m. Kundalini class with Guru Jagat, chanting in a sea of white turbans and Moon Juice drinks; part spiritual practice, part hot social club.

Afternoons could mean Krav Maga sparring with Hollywood stunt hopefuls (I made it to the third belt before I left), dropping into a tantra circle, or wandering Erewhon, a market that is more like a swanky art gallery for produce than a grocery store. Evenings ended with a walk through the Venice Canals, their colorful eye-candy homes glowing at dusk, or a swim in the ocean as the sun went down.

For a time, I felt drenched in inspiration and vitality. It was a life I had built from both desire and courage—until it slipped away. A part of me wondered how it might have continued, if I had been able to stay beyond these years and truly settle into a grounded, long-term life there.

But now it was done.
Probably forever.
Because where was that woman now—did I even care?
I couldn't imagine being her again.

From my seat on the plane, I looked out the window as the ocean shrank beneath me. I held on to the last few moments where I could still make out the boardwalk, could still pick out my street.

Then the view evaporated until all that remained was clouds and sky and the rippling blue waves.

JUNE, 2019: HUNTINGTON, NY

THE CLOSET MELTDOWN

The car pulled up in front of Mom's house just as the sun disappeared behind the roof, glinting orange light through the trees. I was back on Long Island to drop off my LA stuff before quickly returning to Florida. Once we closed out Gabe's apartment, I would come back to our family home indefinitely for the first time since I'd left for college.

The thought of it, along with the three cross-country moves I was juggling, felt like a thousand pounds pressing on my brain. None of these transitions were happy or chosen; they were done in urgency and in grief. To keep from being swallowed by overwhelm, I had to stay with only the moment right in front of me.

I pulled my luggage from the trunk and looked up the driveway at the stone front walk, lined with plants in full summer bloom. This path was the last home renovation my father had planned before he died. I could still picture him standing here in his robe.

My dad, Chuck, had been an animated, hearty guy — welder by day, musician by night — with the broad shoulders, dark beard, and expressive brows of his Sicilian heritage, and the voluminous feathered haircut of the '90s. He was usually humming a tune or telling a funny story, and his hands bore the blackened cracks of metalwork etched into his fingerprints.

But in that final season, illness and time away from welding had shifted his form. He was slender, quieter, the beard gone. His hair had grown longer and wavy, streaked with silver. Those once-marked hands were now washed clean, though they still bore the calluses of a lifelong guitar player.

And he still had the same kind brown eyes.

The porch had become his refuge: zero-gravity chair, boom-box, and his trusty guitar propped against the feeding tube stand. From there, he watched the handyman lay the cement and slate stones one by one. I remembered coming home from college with a stack of CDs so we could listen to the newest bands I loved, and he would usually jam along, acoustic style.

Snapping out of the memory, I took my suitcases and rolled them up the path. The blue stones were cracked and flipped in places, and I needed to be careful while walking. After 15 years, it was time to repair them.

But the hostas spread lushly all the way to the neighboring hydrangeas of indigo and lilac, the ones Mom had planted so Dad would have something colorful to look at on the porch. The wind chimes, now tinged with rust, clanged softly. I got to the front door, found the key behind a potted plant, and stepped inside.

The first thing I saw was what looked like clutter, stacked high on the tiled floor of the den. One bundle was a stack of stamped envelopes bound with rubber bands on a small table—all of the condolence cards that had come to the house so far. Our friend had been picking them up from the mailbox so it wouldn't over-flow. I would read some later, keeping it organized until Mom saw.

Nearby were the things we had kept from Bubbie's apartment, still waiting to be sorted or stored. A reminder that half our imme-diate family had died in three months. That Gabe's tragedy had paused everything else—including the final pieces of Bubbie's life.

I climbed the stairs to the open dining room, where the weathered wooden floor had been painted with exact replicas of the floral wallpaper that stretched up to the skylights. When I was five, Mom had hired someone to paint the floor. I had an early memory of walking out of my room one morning to find the artist lying on her side, cheerfully recreating the pattern.

Hot summer sunlight streamed through the windows, lighting the dust particles as it floated in the beams. It had been a while since anyone had been back here to clean.

The old, untuned piano sat like a family memorial more than an instrument. It was covered in framed photos from every era: My grandparents as newlyweds, my uncles laughing at Mom's high school graduation party, and a birth announcement that my great-grandfather had hand-drawn in the 1940s. Gabe and I in homemade Joker costumes and back-to-school pictures with James and Sean. Our family pets: silver cat Hazel and mini-dachshund Chas, both gone but never forgotten.

Next to that picture was an enlarged photo of my brother from a couple years ago when he and Maskell sat court-side for his beloved Knicks. After the game, Gabe laid on the court of Madison Square Garden in his Patrick Ewing jersey, arms and legs outstretched like he was making snow angels, eyes closed in bliss.

The photos with Gabe in them left me tight and angry, a raw feeling from being flooded with too many images at once of my brother alive and well.

At the top of the stairs was a white bedroom door with a Christmas ornament I made in nursery school still hanging from the knob. That had been my bedroom growing up. Gabe's was just down the hall. But over the years, Mom converted his room into a wardrobe for her shoes and accessories, and my old room became the guest room. Our parent's bedroom remained at the far end of the hallway.

Even though it was my ornament on the door, the room inside had become my brother's. After ending his engagement and recovering from surgery, he'd moved home for a while. This was where he stayed before spontaneously heading down to Miami.

For the last year and a half, when I came to visit, I'd slept on a cot in the den. That suited me fine. Gabe needed the room, and I preferred the feeling of impermanence when I was visiting here, anyway. Too many unresolved feelings and memories.

I set my bags at the bottom of the stairs and paused with the quiet of the house. The sky was darkening. Somewhere far off, a neighbor's lawnmower buzzed.

I didn't want to go into the room, but I had to start making space. I still had boxes and suitcases coming back from LA and they would need to go somewhere.

So I walked up the stairs and opened the door with the Christmas ornament.

My bedroom still had some hints of me; the walls painted in my favorite shade of blue, the black and white zebra-print carpeting, a few of my watercolors framed on the wall and some of my favorite CDs from high school on a shelf.

But otherwise, it was all Gabe.

His books and journals lined the rest of the shelves. His extra socks, underwear, and T-shirts filled the drawers. In the dresser's old TV alcove, he'd made a healing altar: crystals, photos, and written intentions for recovery. On the desk, Gabe's post-surgery eye patch and a prescription for pain meds still lay untouched.

As I looked around, my skin felt itchy, I started to sweat and my heart beat fast. I felt trapped and miserable. This wasn't like walking into his Miami apartment, which had once felt like freedom and possibility. This small room felt oppressive and even claustrophobic

Especially now, packed with artifacts of Gabe's final recovery. The one that hadn't saved him.

Recovering so well, only to die anyway, I thought bitterly.

I opened the overstuffed closet. His formal winter clothes were still in there; suits, sweaters, coats. Not needed in Miami's spring heat, but now not needed at all.

This is where I would start.

I lugged a plastic storage bin into the room from the hallway and pushed it against the wall.

Piece by piece, I pulled Gabe's clothing off the rack. Beautifully tailored suits, lavender and blue dress shirts, brown argyle sweaters, black wool dress pants, and supple leather dress shoes with stylish thin laces. I picked up the clothes selectively at first and then more manically, my arms full of all of Gabe's nicest outfits.

A wardrobe tailored for wedding receptions, important meetings, and elegant dinners.

He should still need them.

I tossed the first load into the bottom of the barrel and watched it all unceremoniously crumple into a heap. It felt like I had taken a beautifully decorated layer cake off its silver platter and smashed into the frosting with both fists.

Wrong wrong wrong.

I hated that these clothes were not needed anymore. I hated that they could be donated or sold or set on fucking fire, because Gabe would never wear any of it again. All his care and taste, reduced to nothing. The wool fabric and the sharp plastic edges of the bin scratched my arms as I grabbed and tossed, feeling as if my chest was caving in on me.

When the closet was empty, I dropped to the floor and sobbed.

I clutched my chest. The pain was *physical*, waves of agony radiating and wild. For a moment the pain was so great I thought it might kill me.

After a few horrible minutes, I steadied my breath and crawled to the bed, grabbing my phone.

Who can I call?

There were friends who had shown up in the past, but I was afraid. Afraid to overwhelm them; that this would be the thing that hit their limit and pushed them away. Everyone seemed so busy, and my grief felt too loud to interrupt their lives.

It was a strange new feeling—embarrassment.

I couldn't remember being this concerned with how I'd be perceived, at least not since Jr. High. But now it pulsed beneath the surface, warning me not to expose too much while I was still this fragile. In that foggy, grief-drenched logic, I told myself a story:

They're probably back to their own lives.
Maybe people will be around again when we have the memorial

That wouldn't be until we were officially back home in July.

Some of the friends I'd expected to lean on had already begun to pull away. They responded to calls with care packages or texts—kind gestures, but not what I needed. Not in those moments when I was desperate for someone to answer the phone and remind me of who I had been before this. Then, the silence was deafening.

Maybe it was too scary. Maybe they were too uneasy about what they'd feel or be asked to faced if they picked up. On some level, I understood. But it didn't lessen the pain.

Time might repair some connections, but not all. I would never need people the way I needed them now. And for once, it couldn't be reciprocal. Had Gabe not died, I might never have known which friendships would quietly unravel under pressure. Maybe we could have stayed close forever. But the dissolution had already begun. And like so many other things that were here until suddenly they weren't, some relationships had an expiration date: the day my brother died.

I had read in a grief book that this was called "secondary loss," the unexpected endings that follow the primary death. It was normal enough to warrant its own term, and yet I still burned with sorrow for not having seen these losses coming—and with shame for how much it hurt, even with what had just happened to Gabe.

*Shouldn't his death eclipse **everything** else?*

121

But it reminded me of when Dad died. I was still upset over friend drama and unrequited crushes. Back then, I chalked it up to being a college kid. Now I knew better.

Even as an adult, I was learning that some friendships couldn't exist outside the version of me who was easier to be around. *Fun.* Tender feelings were fine if unearthed during a workshop or retreat; something you could release into the circle before heading out to dinner. Supporting someone through real-time tragedy was different. And not everyone was up for it.

It also turned out that *I* wasn't up for helping them find their way back to me. Not this time, not even to save the friendship.

I threw down my phone in frustration.

So many friends, a successful healing career. A network of coaches and practitioners. And in that moment, I couldn't think of one person I felt safe calling in this much pain.

All of it—my striving, my self-work, my identity—suddenly seemed like a total failure. I felt victimized by my every choice.

What had I even been *doing* with my life if I had nobody to call?

I slid down the wall to the corner of the room. Even the suit-case couldn't fit. It lay against the bedroom door, waiting outside like a sleeping dog. I cried. A steady, pelting rain into my arms.

Then something in me shifted. I zoomed out and saw the room from above.

I'm alone and trapped in this house that triggers me, in a bedroom I hate, throwing Gabe's suits into a bin.
It's like I'm in a movie, except no one else will ever see or feel this moment. And I just can't believe I have to do this alone.

Ten minutes later, I had no strength left to cry, but what came next was sober clarity. There *would be* other times to call people who could pick up, moments where my pain would be witnessed and held by others. But this time would not be one of them, and that's why I couldn't feel who to call.

This was my bedroom.

This was my closet.

This was my brother.

As excruciating as it was, the simple fact of that crystallized this scene into a memory that went beyond the agony into the truth:

We can't be rescued from the suffering that's ours to experience. Nobody else was meant to be there, because this was mine to do. It was *my* heart that was meant to break—and maybe one day, my strength and power to own.

JUNE, 2019: MIAMI BEACH, FL

THE GOODBYE BRUNCH

"*O*h my God, you're gonna have us locked in here *forever!*"

I was laughing and crying at the same time, delirious with exhaustion. It was the last day of June, and we were down to the final minutes of our time in Gabe's apartment. But now, the front door was stuck. No amount of pulling or pushing would open it.

It was the perfect finale to four nonstop, crazy-making days.

Sean had kindly flown in to help with the move-out. We'd spent the past three days taping up boxes and sorting through every last piece of minutiae: refrigerator magnets, toothpaste, shoe racks. We bubble-wrapped Gabe's TV and loaded his new mattress, couch, and chairs into a rental van, running back and forth through the Florida downpours. Only one legendary fall, courtesy of Sean and a slick curb.

April joined us for multiple trips to Aunt Rosemary's storage unit, where we placed Gabe's items in increasingly creative Tetris arrangements. The facility was above a Subway sandwich shop, and the combined gritty scent of old metal and freshly baked bread made me cover my nose every time we pulled up.

In total, we gave some things away, stored others, and managed to reduce it all to what we could fit into Gabe's car—which Mom and I would be driving back to Long Island in a trip I'd already confidently titled, *The Road Trip to and from Hell*.

We kept our heads down, pushing through the brutal humidity and the even heavier weight of grief. Mom came and went, fluttering around and finding other errands to run. It was too painful for her to watch Gabe's beautiful new chapter be dismantled piece by piece.

I had grown agitated and isolated staying in this apartment but for Mom, it had been a solace.

"This is where I can feel him," she told me softly one day as we looked out at the bay, just beyond the pool. "We *just* put this place together with him. I'm not ready for it to be over yet."

On our last night, we ordered all our favorites from Puerto Sagua and sat on the bare floor, eating the morose and plantains off paper plates. The kitchen table was already gone.

In the morning, Sean and I did a final sweep. Meanwhile, Mom poured her energy into what she does best: creating ritual events to mark big transitions.

On this note, she decided to throw a goodbye brunch for the building staff.

Around ten AM, she came through the door frazzled but determined, her arms filled with shopping bags full of muffins, bagels, shmears, orange juice, a giant box of coffee, and the corresponding paper goods.

We brought it all downstairs to the break room, just down the hall from where Gabe had collapsed.

By this point, I was feeling burnt out and more than a little self-conscious about the whole thing. Wasn't it bizarre to be making a "goodbye party" for the staff of the building where my brother had lived for nine weeks before his sudden and tragic passing in the gym?

*What are we even **doing**?* I thought with frustration, as I continued to arrange the bagels in a circular pattern around the containers of cream cheese, shaping them into a floral design. The plating instinct was second nature after years of hosting, even though I was sick of being the family everyone looked at with pity. But as I watched Mom gently set out napkins and juice cups with care, my irritation softened. I recognized how important this was.

This was how she held and then alchemized the pain.

This was our way.

"*Dark Times Catering* strikes again," I whispered with a shrug.

The name had been born after one of many memorial events we threw; gatherings full of music, food, photos, joy, and heartbreak. Someone had once joked that we should start a company.

"Call us the *Dark Times Caterers*," Mom had replied dryly.

Now it was our private punchline.

Mom walked out of the room and into the front desk area. "Okay," she called out brightly. "Breakfast is ready!"

The staff slowly and solemnly walked into the room. I wondered what they thought this was—a funeral? A macabre Bon Voyage? A creative way to be legally served with a lawsuit for not having a cardiac defibrillator in the building?

Everyone smiled politely while they plated their meal. I imagined the internal monologues:

Isn't this the family of that friendly young guy who died in the gym? Are they really... serving us **breakfast?**

They just didn't know about the **Dark Times Caterers** yet.

They didn't know this was Mom's way of saying thank you: for the kindness, for baring witness, for being part of her son's story and final home. This was giving reverence for the spiritual truth that Gabe's soul had chosen this place and these people for his last two months of life.

It was how we said goodbye to what should have been.

The leasing agent and front desk woman entered, giving us

warm hugs and handing Mom a bouquet of bright yellow sunflowers—Gabe's favorite. The same flowers he brought to the desk every Friday morning he'd lived there.

"He was just the *nicest*," one said. "We already loved having him here."

Two maintenance men sat off to the side, eating quietly. I noticed they were looking at Mom and me, as if they wanted to say something but were holding back.

After everyone was served, we went upstairs to finish the last of the packing. Sean stood by the window, gaze distant, the weight of it all catching up to him. Mom moved to open the front door, but it wouldn't budge, and she started to panic at the feeling of being closed in on.

"It's stuck!" she cried, pulling harder.

We came over, trying to shove and pry the door open. Nothing worked. It felt symbolic to all of us—would we ever get out of this crazy time and back into our own lives?

I called downstairs. It took a few tries for anyone to answer, since, ironically, they were still in the break room having bagels. Finally, the front desk picked up and said Maintenance would come up shortly.

A few minutes later, after fiddling unsuccessfully with the locks, they yelled through the door that they were removing it from its hinges. Soon we were all standing face to face in the now-open doorway, a hot breeze rushing past their bright blue uniforms.

It was the two men at brunch, the ones who had seemed like they wanted to say something. One stepped forward, gesturing to his colleague, whose eyes brimmed with tears.

"He doesn't speak English," he said. "But we...we were there. We've always wanted to tell you what happened."

They were the ones who had tried to revive Gabe in the gym before the paramedics arrived.

There were no chairs left, so we all stood for the kind of

conversation you'd want to be sitting down for. The man spoke in Spanish, wiping tears from his eyes, while his colleague translated in halting English. The broken phrases came in pieces, and this was a blessing—any more detail would have been too much to take in.

They told us that another resident had been in the gym when Gabe collapsed on the treadmill. They ran out, calling for help. The men rushed in, found him, and began CPR. The paramedics arrived soon after, but he never regained consciousness. Then he was taken to the hospital.

It matched what I had received intuitively in the early days:

I was there, and then I was gone. I didn't feel anything. I was already on my way out.

Mom looked up, her voice soft, her eyes sad. She sighed and said,

"Thank you. I've wanted to know, and I'm glad he wasn't alone."

There was a security camera in the gym that had recorded the incident. The detective who came to the scene later told us about it, but he'd warned us plainly:

"It's up to you, but you can't unsee something like that."

We chose not to watch. There were already enough hard things to see.

Both men wiped their eyes, and the translator added quietly,

"We didn't know him long, but he was special."

"Yes," Mom said, her voice catching. "He was just the greatest person."

When they left, I felt grateful it had been them—not close friends, who would have been deeply traumatized, but still not strangers. They were kind people, and they knew him.

I remembered Gabe's first days in the apartment, realizing it was those same men laughing with him as they fixed the ceiling fan and assembled his TV stand.

"I love those guys," Gabe had said. "So nice, and they can help you put together anything."

For all his brilliance, my brother was not exactly handy. James and Sean used to call him Tom Sawyer for his knack at enlisting others to help with practical tasks. As an adult, he was simply happy to pay generously for the help.

"And they said they'll be around whenever I need them," he'd added with a smile.

After Sean left for the airport, we headed to Aunt Rosemary's for her birthday dinner. The Hidden Arches crew were gathered in the formal dining room. We'd promised to attend, and now that we were leaving, it felt important to be there. It was hard to imagine coming back for a visit anytime soon.

The room buzzed with strained joviality when we walked in. I felt the energy shift—or maybe that was my own projection. I tried to smile, then realized I couldn't even imagine making small talk.

I sat down on a brocade dining chair, my legs still damp from a quick shower. Dizzy from packing and hauling so much in the heat, I sipped water and tried to focus on the meal. A platter of glossy BBQ chicken sat in the center of the table, along with rice and beans, coleslaw, and a cherry pie like a full moon.

I forked a bite of chicken with slaw, but nausea rolled through me. I put the fork down. Aunt Rosemary looked across the table.

"How'd it go, Al? I know how hard you must have worked."

I nodded, eyes filling with tears.

"Well," she whispered, "I think you're very brave."

"Thanks," I said hoarsely.

The tears fell freely now. I stood quickly, my chair scraping across the tile, and ran into the front hallway bathroom with the blue chandelier and pee pads for Marco. I locked the door and vomited.

Two days later, after I'd recovered from the heatstroke that had made me sick, it was time for the drive to the auto-train station. And we were late. Mom was yelling, her grief and the unbearable weather had transmuted into frustration. She wore red-and-white boat shoes someone had given her—an attempt at manual labor footwear. It was a sharp left turn from her usual glittery flip-flops or finely woven espadrilles.

I watched the shoes stomp down the stone-filled walkway, dust rising in the sweltering air.

"Mom," I said dryly, "I just can't take you seriously in these dumb shoes. From the ankles down it's like watching a tiny sailor have a tantrum."

She paused. Then chuckled. The tension broke.

Dad and Gabe had always known how to do this—diffuse Mom's fiery moods with humor and gentle mocking; never hurtful, always finding the laugh in the moment. I, in contrast, had always yelled back or disconnected—unwilling to let comments roll off, angry at feeling misunderstood.

But now it seemed I had inherited this gift. I imagined it like a sparkly green light passed from Gabe to me. My brother's presence flowing through me, teaching me how to hold the tension like he did. Suddenly I could execute plans, calm Mom down, and create levity.

I was the man of the house now.

He would have known this would be the hardest part—for Mom and for me. The soft, loving energy of Bubbie, and then the comedic relief, compassion, and masculine protection we once had in Dad and Gabe, was missing from our family.

And now—suddenly—it was just us. The female caregivers, finally learning how to care for ourselves, and maybe, for each other.

The final text I ever got from Gabe was the last response in a longer conversation. Simple, but profound:

The Universe is giving you an opportunity.

We'd been talking about the current dynamics, about how I was frustrated I couldn't have more space from our mother and family stuff until I was feeling more on top of things. But now, there was *no* separation. No hiding. No one else to shield or serve. Just Mom and me. And this, I knew, was the opportunity Gabe's soul had meant in that text.

Even if neither of us had asked for it.

JULY, 2019: SOMEWHERE IN FLORIDA

THE ROAD TRIP TO & FROM HELL

"*O*kay, just keep your hands on the wheel and look straight ahead. They're professionals, so I don't *think* they're going to hit us?"

Mom shook her head and kept white-knuckling the steering wheel of the Subaru as we barreled along the highway, somehow in the center of a mystery formation of race cars. I sat next to her, gripping my phone as the chipper robot-woman voice directed us to stay on this road for the next 27 miles.

We were surrounded by race cars so bright they were almost offensive—electric blues, neon greens, hot pinks. They zigzagged back and forth, flooding the air with a sound like a million wasps. A sickly yellow car flew past us, plastered with images of sandwiches and SUBWAY printed across the hood in bold green.

"Christ, we're on the same travel route as the Daytona 500."

I rubbed my eyes to stay present, aware that Mom's stress was mounting. The air was blistering, rippling off the hood in visible waves. The A/C hummed loudly, struggling to cool us as the smell of burned rubber poured through the vents. I was practically glued to my seat with sweat, balancing Gabe's urn carefully on my lap.

The Road Trip to and from Hell was officially underway.

I wanted to shift into a more comfortable position, but there was nowhere safer to put the urn. Every square inch of my brother's vehicle was packed. On the bottom, two large suitcases were filled with his Miami wardrobe—polo shirts, khaki shorts, linen button-downs, swim trunks, leather flip-flops, and a beloved collection of baseball caps.

There was a box of his crystals and books next to a bin of kitchenware, including his Vitamix and collection of dry spices. Then came my travel bag, Mom's suitcase, and finally, Gabe's collection of plants: five new tropicals and one old faithful—a 25-year-old curling ivy in a small terracotta pot. The newer plants were so tall and lush from the rain that they poked through the open sunroof.

I kept trying to ground myself as the race cars roared around us. Finally, they sped ahead and exited off the highway towards Daytona, their sound fading until all of the cars were mercifully gone. Mom and I let out a collective breath. The ridiculousness of the moment finally registered.

"You can't make this up. Anything insane that *can* happen to us, *does*," Mom laughed.

"How are race cars even allowed to do that?!" I exclaimed.

Just as the highway turned relatively peaceful, Mom veered towards a new exit for 3Gs Deli in Delray Beach. It was a sacred Jewish food stop she simply could not pass up; a split-second decision in pursuit of their famous turkey sandwich. Over my protests about running late she proclaimed:

"You know there's not going to be anything I can eat on that train. It'll only take a minute!"

She was probably right. Mom was highly allergic to butter and could smell it like a bloodhound. You'd be shocked how many foods contain it without listing it, or how often dishes are cooked with it even after being told of the allergy. We always joked she'd have made an excellent poison-tester for a king.

Inside 3Gs, Florida retirees filled the booths, spooning coleslaw and flipping laminated menus while waiters balanced trays of bagels and pastrami on rye. I stood by the register, tapping one foot. I wanted Mom to have food, but I was worried about our tight timeline and the long drive to the train station still ahead of us. I hated running late, especially for travel. Growing up, it felt like my parents never left on time.

"You know us Hoffmans, we like a bit of chaos," they'd say cheerfully.

Mom was at the glass bakery case, delighted by the nostalgia of black-and-white cookies, rugelach, and Joyva jelly rings.

"They have the mini halvahs!" she beamed.

As we got back on the highway, she popped a chocolate-covered jelly ring in her mouth. "You'll see. You'll be so glad we have this."

Four hours later, we sat by the tracks watching as everyone else settled into their seats through the small square windows. The conductor was sweating through his light-blue uniform as he told us pleasantly:

"Sorry, ladies, we have a firm cut-off time of forty-five minutes before taking off. If you're not there for the start of boarding, you are not allowed to board. No rushing on!"

I gave my mother a pointed look as I asked the conductor faux-innocently:

"Oh, so like, you can't just jump on the train last-minute?"

"Nope," he chuckled as he started to walk away. "But the good news is you can get on our very next train. It heads out this time tomorrow!"

I dropped my bag at my feet with a groan.

I just wanted to get out of this godforsaken state. But Florida had its clammy grip on me via heatstroke and turkey salad.

We trudged back to the car. I leaned against the door, feeling the metal sear through my sundress.

"Well, I...guess we weren't meant to go on that one?" Mom offered, cautiously.

I looked at her, still clutching the paper bag.

"Oh, you better eat the *hell* out of that sandwich," I said. "I hope it's the best sandwich of your life. You and 3Gs are officially on my shit list."

We burst into peals of laughter at the absurdity of it all. I quickly found a nearby hotel on Priceline and set Google Maps to get us there. Mom turned the car back on, Beatles Sirius station playing us into the sunset.

We were finding a rhythm now, the two of us. There was nowhere to hide.

At the hotel, I grabbed a rickety luggage cart and began the first of several trips to unload the car, plants and all. We had to bring them in; the sunroof needed to be closed for the incoming storm.

Once in our room for the night, we each sat on a twin bed with one half of the sandwich. It was fine. Not worth a 24-hour delay, but good enough. We opened the minibar— Mom popped a tiny bottle of champagne, I grabbed peanut M&Ms, and we watched *Big Little Lies* while rain pattered outside into the small hotel pool where kids played on, unfazed. They were not about to let the weather ruin their fun.

By the next evening, we were finally aboard the train, take two. I sat in a hard vinyl seat bolted to the floor, rocking with the rhythm as the train moved north. Mom sat beside me. Opposite us were our dining companions—assigned strangers, as per Amtrak dinner service custom.

The table had a white polyester cloth draped over the fake wood surface, a tiny vase of yellow flowers, and a bread basket with foil cubes of butter.

"Okay, let's go around and say our names and why we're on the train!" the woman across from us chirped. She wore a Disney shirt with Ursula the sea witch from *The Little Mermaid* on it, and had the sunburn-meets-suntan look of a Florida vacation. I could guess where she was coming back from.

Usually I'd be game but not this time.

Mom responded quickly. "We're helping a relative move out of their apartment, bringing their car and things home."

I kept my eyes on the little plate in front. I was struggling with the still-cold butter; it was tearing the bread apart when I tried to spread it.

The older man beside Disney Queen scoffed. "No offense, but I don't like to converse at the table."

Bless this grumpy man, I thought.

The unanswered questions hung in the air, and at that moment the food was delivered. Mom switched into autopilot to chat briefly with the woman, playing the game of keep-away we were often immersed in lately, particularly when speaking to people who didn't know us.

They had no idea—how could they?—that the most innocuous-seeming questions could burst open the dam and bring forth a monstrous wave of sadness. Then we would have to hold their discomfort with our pain, faces wincing, shifting our voices to become grief diplomats with a smooth:

"Thank you, yeah, it's very sad . . ." as they piled on their mortified condolences for ever asking *anything* in the first place.

Later that night, I twisted in my seat, trying to sleep. Mom and the others snored softly while the South Carolina forests blurred by in the dark. By morning, we'd reach the final stop outside D.C., retrieve the car and begin the last leg of the trip to Huntington, NY.

So much was waiting there. The boxes I'd shipped from California, the suitcases I had dropped off in my room that awful weekend, all of Gabe's medical records and business taxes, Bubbie's belongings, the memorial planning. And a house filled with echoes of absence.

Huntington, a leafy Long Island suburb an hour's ride from

New York City, had its charms. There were historic houses with plaques noting where George Washington once stopped for a pint, and a lively downtown with a beloved bookstore that hosted famous authors, a great concert hall, a renowned cinema arts center, and plenty of restaurants and bars.

Along the water was the dock with its old-school deli, where you could grab a bacon-egg-and-cheese on a roll and watch the sailboats and fishing rigs pass. I could follow West Neck Road to the peaceful rocky beach, or keep going with the Long Island Sound glittering to my left, until I reached Caumsett Historic State Park, with its beautiful trees. Or I could take the train just minutes from our house, a straight shot to Penn Station.

But while I had liked Huntington Village as a kid and tween, I'd been turning from my hometown since leaving for college 17 years earlier. Most of my friends who had lost a parent young had done the same: built lives far away from their first one.

For those of us in that club, returning didn't offer the comfort it seemed to give others, whose visits weren't shadowed by the memory of a hospice bed, or an empty chair at the kitchen table, or a house that felt quieter than it should. I wasn't sure how I would face Gabe becoming the next empty seat in our own home.

But at least we were done with Florida.

No more staying in a posh building that now felt like tragedy instead of a fresh start. No more once-magical manatees that had become big sputtering reminders of how I couldn't save my brother. No more sweltering heat, chaotic highways, frowning people in the elevator, turkey sandwiches, or rolling luggage carts through the rain.

I wiped my tears, adjusted my shoulder against the window, turned up the music in my headphones, and tried to find comfort in that.

JULY 2019 HUNTINGTON, NY

THE FUNERAL

"*I*'ve actually never been to a funeral before," the man said.

He was the new boyfriend of a dear friend of Gabe's, and I had to lean in to hear him over the babbling of water from the angel-statue fountain. The sound mingled with the 90s Italian ballads booming from speakers placed around the room.

Waiters moved briskly, balancing trays of marinated artichokes, olives, and prosciutto. Behind the open kitchen, a white-mustached man—who had worked the wood-burning oven for as long as anyone could remember—expertly slid pizza pies from the flames, slicing them into perfect thin triangles. A waitress placed the plates on long tables adorned with flowers, framed photographs, and bright place settings.

My eyes widened in response to his statement. I wondered what it would be like to *not* be so intimately familiar with death's rituals. To attend a funeral for the first time as an adult, rather than as a memorial hostess with the mostess.

I smiled wryly. "The next one might be a little different."

The three of us looked around the restaurant: Joanina's, a beloved rustic Italian spot in Huntington Village. We'd been coming here for family gatherings and celebrations for decades, and I had even waited tables here for a year after college. It embodied the true spirit of that Olive Garden slogan: *"When you're here, you're family."* When I called the owners with my plan for a communal dinner to close our the day of Gabe's memorial, they immediately began arranging it. They set up the banquet room, where we had once celebrated Bubbie's 90th birthday.

This setting was a far cry from what was usually depicted as a funeral in movies: a group of mourners in black, umbrellas shielding them from rain, standing somberly around a grave. Then a stiff reception with barely touched casseroles. Finally, nightfall— the main griever sits alone in a big empty house, loss echoing through the stillness.

But this was decidedly *not* that.

This was a space filled with warmth, nourishment, and life. The memorial and reception were behind us, and now we gathered for a dinner with close friends, family, and those who had traveled in. By this point in the day, we had crossed the most daunting thresholds: speeches given with shaking hands, the weight of the unknown finally revealed and released.

At last, we could settle into the relief of being with loved ones more casually. The evening was a chance to gather our favorite moments from the day and to enjoy a beautiful meal in Gabe's honor. By dinnertime, the tears had mostly dried, and laughter became the cathartic release that carried us through the night. Guests chose their seats, hugged people they hadn't seen in a while, and dropped into conversation over bright, bubbling Aperol Spritzes. I could almost see Gabe sitting at the head of the table; these were the sort of gatherings he loved.

I felt proud to witness what we had created as a community. The memorial had fulfilled its intention: a healing experience and energetic attunement worthy of Gabe's legacy—something to support all of us in stepping into the next phase.

The day began at St. John's Church, the same place where we had held Dad's memorial fifteen years earlier. Ever since, it had felt like sacred ground. Built nearly two centuries ago of white wood, the church still bears its original welcome sign from 1835. It rests beside a wide pond and nature preserve, home to swans, ducks, turtles, and a stand of ancient trees that whisper in the breeze. Just next door is the fish hatchery and aquarium we all visited on elementary school field trips.

Inside, the church was lined with dark wood and red velvet, its Tiffany stained-glass windows casting rainbow light across pews that had held generations of stories, including ours, though we had never been formal members. Mom had grown up Jewish, and Dad had been, famously, the youngest Catholic altar boy on Long Island. My brother and I inherited traditions from both.

Our family cherished the beauty of the place until loss called us here, first for Dad and then, fifteen years later, for Gabe. At first, we weren't sure they would even allow us to hold our services there, let alone bring in a full rock band for both memorials. But they did. The reverend who welcomed our first request in 2004 turned out to be a music lover, and he remembered us when we called again fifteen years later.

I had been absorbed in the final details since our return to Huntington two weeks earlier. Each day I stopped at Kinko's, printing and framing photos of Gabe with friends and family until the staff knew me by name. Mom and I reserved catering for the reception, managed travel and lodging logistics, and tried to balance sensitivities—who would be comfortable where, who needed what—in a town with almost no real hotels.

For the memorial program, I used Dad's as a template but shifted it into something that felt more like Gabe. Instead of a traditional religious prayer card, I designed a business-style card in the aqua shade he loved, with a photo from our final visit and a favorite Joseph Campbell quote on one side:

"We must let go of the life we have planned, so as to accept the one that is waiting for us."

On the other side, I paired his kindergarten school picture—his face lit with a precious smile—with a line he often offered when someone was upset or overwhelmed:

"One step at a time."

The out-of-town arrivals began the day before. I picked up Anne at the airport after one last Kinko's run. We blasted Y2K Hits on Sirius and, for a brief moment, it felt like we were just two girls cruising on summer break.

"Stop at Walgreens!" Anne suddenly blurted. "I'm getting cigarettes. It's going to be an intense weekend."

Then she hesitated, her voice turning serious. "I swear I feel Gabe here. And he's saying skip the cigarettes... and get a pregnancy test."

"Anne!" I yelped, swerving toward the parking lot. "Are you for real?" She nodded slowly.

An hour later, back at Mom's house, I heard the bathroom door creak open. Anne stepped out smiling and shaking her head.

"Oh. Wow," she said, stunned. "It's positive. I need to call my husband!"

I smiled, blinking back tears as I wrapped her in a hug. Just on the other side of that wall was Gabe's old bedroom, which somehow made it feel even more special that Anne had discovered her long-hoped-for pregnancy here. My brother would have pulled her into a proud hug of his own.

And still, the final hurdles appeared: train delays with unexpected detours for those traveling in from New York City, and the forecast of this being the hottest day of the *year*. This very old church did not have much air conditioning, and by 7:30 a.m. it was already 85 degrees.

I sat with the discomfort of asking others to be uncomfortable at something hosted by our family, in honor of Gabe. We couldn't rescue anyone, not from the logistics, not from the heat, not from the grief. Not even ourselves.

When I arrived early, I took a moment alone to pray before starting set-up. I asked to stay open to the unfolding of this day, rather than bracing myself against everything I could not control.

Just then, Dr. Izzo, one of Gabe's longtime mentors, walked in. He placed a hand on my back, and the dam broke. I cried quietly for a few minutes as he stood beside me, holding space. That was enough. The memorial would be something I would carry with me for the rest of my life—and just for today, I wanted to hold it not only for myself, but for everyone. There was a distinct honor and privilege in having so many people join us in celebrating our favorite person.

Four hundred people filled St. John's. The band was made up of my uncle and my dad's lifelong friends and bandmates, people who had been playing together for decades and had watched Gabe and me grow up. We began with a grounding meditation, followed multiple speakers: a tapestry of stories and songs, woven through with both laughter and tears.

I introduced each speaker until it was my own turn. When I thought about what to say, I realized it didn't feel right to speak much about my relationship with Gabe. I wouldn't have even known where to begin; the event itself spoke to that. Instead, I chose to acknowledge what we had all overcome just to be there— the emotional, physical, and logistical hurdles. What did it mean that a day already *so* hard carried these extra challenges?

"I realize we have all been in the fire today," I said, as Mom tossed mini bottles of water into the crowd like we were at a rock concert.

"But something I think we can all acknowledge about Gabe was that he *himself* was often in the fire; dealing with compression and intensity, more than we could have known, and he just kept going. He kept showing up. Today, we showed up, too. We endured the fire to celebrate his life. Because our love for Gabe pulled us forward. And we're becoming who we must be without him. Who we *can* be, because he was in our lives."

I sensed the room begin to soften into the heat. People were still mopping their brows, but, I hoped, settling into the shared experience—challenges included.

After the speeches came practices Gabe held dear, many of them new to those gathered. Dr. Izzo led a crystal bowl meditation, followed by Cameron, one of Gabe's close friends from his Qigong training, who guided a gentle movement practice. I looked out into a sea of people, eyes closed, hands floating softly in front of them. Even the new reverend, who had resisted *much* of the non-traditional planning, had joined in. She opened her eyes and smiled at me before returning to stillness. This small exchange was something Gabe would have loved.

The band returned for one last song, and everyone stood with arms around each other, swaying, and singing along to the final number *"Lean on Me"* by Bill Withers. It was beautiful.

Afterward, we filed into the reception room, which was blissfully cooler. The local families that made up our longtime community brought platters of food and ice buckets filled with bottles of lemonade and sparkling wine. Uncle Marty created a slideshow of Gabe through the years. Sean made a playlist of Gabe's favorite hip-hop and R&B: Jay-Z, 112, Pharcyde, Drake, Ludacris.

The vibe was lit. It felt like we'd just put on a brilliant show—because we had. A co-created soulful offering, by *and* for Gabe.

I watched the two sides of his life merge. Those unfamiliar with meditation, crystal bowls, or energy work were moved, or even surprised by how much they enjoyed it, as many later told me. Others who had only known Gabe through his more stoic or spiritual pursuits seemed delighted to discover his equal passion for sports, comedy, and road trips, to hear stories of the man who made women swoon with both his heart and his humor.

Gabe contained multitudes, and we gave all of him space to shine in our remembrance.

That night, some of Gabe's friends continued to the local bars, but I was spent. I headed to a sleepover at the Airbnb my Chicago friends had rented. When I got there, I was nothing short of *stunned.*

A surly white parrot sat in a cage on the front porch, straight out of a pirate movie.

"GET OUTTA HERE!" it squawked repeatedly.

Upstairs, we found a one-bedroom apartment which the owner had listed as a "three-bedroom house." This, apparently, was because they had placed beds in both the kitchen *and* the bathroom.

Every wall was wallpapered in psychedelic neon patterns. The moldings? Carefully wrapped in tinfoil. **Why?!**

"Uh, you guys? What did this look like online?" I asked, eyes wide.

"Well, listen—there was basically nothing available in your town," Anne defended. "We were trying to stay close. And...it's not that bad. It's...charming?" She was already laughing.

Even stranger was the host's name on the listing.

"Will *Sorrentino?*" I yelled.

Will had been in Gabe's grade in high school. He'd played the French horn in marching band.

We scrolled through his combative replies to negative reviews of his bizarre apartment:

> NOT TRUE! Classic case of someone who couldn't follow house rules!

Delirious from heat, emotion, and exhaustion, I collapsed onto one of the beds with the rest of my friends. We laughed so hard we cried, as we read the reviews aloud.

I knew more grief and distance was coming. But that day we had created something worthy and true—full of love, friendship, healing, and the celebration of Gabe and what mattered most to him. And I would let myself have that.

JULY, 2019: MANHATTAN, NY

THE BIG MEETING

*W*e sat at a long, glossy table and waited.

The room was sleek, encased in glass walls and lined with floor-to-ceiling medical textbooks bound in burgundy, royal purple, and brown leather. Through the glass, people moved briskly in and out of offices, absorbed in their work and unaware of the profound loss that had brought us here.

The door opened, and we looked up expectantly.

Here we go, I whispered to myself.

Gabe had dared to believe he was in good hands with the head of cardiology at a prestigious hospital. But it was devastatingly clear now that he had been misled. His cardiologist assured him at their final appointment there was nothing to worry about. The minor valve issues they had detected, he said, were still years away from needing any intervention.

Any other symptoms, he suggested, were simply side effects of anxiety to work through. He reassured Gabe that if something more serious were at play, it would have already shown up on their scans.

That morning, Mom had asked to join Gabe at the appointment, nudged by a feeling she couldn't shake. When she voiced her unease during the visit, she was casually brushed aside.

"Don't worry so much," they told her.

The doctors my brother had entrusted told him to set aside any worries and trust their expertise. They said it was time to move on, even recommending a treadmill walking program to rebuild confidence in his cardiac stamina. He had begun right away at the gym in his new apartment building—doctor's orders.

In the aftermath, we were told it was both a miracle and a testament to his otherwise good health that Gabe hadn't suffered a heart attack sooner. A serious cardiac condition had been brewing all along, likely connected to the radiation he'd received during cancer treatment as a teenager.

It should have been caught and treated. The very tests that might have revealed this had never been ordered. Instead, reassured by their scans and their confidence, Gabe followed advice that allowed the worst-case scenario to unfold.

The truth of the oversight was finally visible, just far too late to save my brother.

Rage flared through me, bright and hot like lava. It needed somewhere to *go*, something to transform into. The sorrow was beyond words, knowing this had been Gabe's experience. To imagine how he might have felt each day, given how serious his condition truly was, was horrifying.

For someone who had devoted his life to health, healing, and helping others, the betrayal felt especially crushing. Gabe's life had been lost to negligence, and the least we could do was seek some measure of accountability.

I wore the black jumpsuit and white robe with red blossoms from Gabe's memorial. Around my neck hung his red jasper mala beads. Mom sat beside me in the lavender-gray dress from his cremation ceremony, her stone bracelets clinking softly as she adjusted them. Around her neck, a silver pendant holding Gabe's ashes.

Kenny, a longtime family friend and accomplished Manhattan lawyer, sat with us, offering calm and clarity. He had generously offered to come along and help translate the legal complexity.

It was our first meeting with a top-tier malpractice firm. With no legal experience between us, it felt intimidating—but we'd gotten this far with the help of our community. Cousins who worked in law, friends in medicine, and other trusted allies had helped us build the confidence to walk into these rooms. Asking for help was vulnerable, but our need for justice was greater.

The door opened. A tall, suntanned man—from his boat, he would later explain—entered, dressed in a sharp suit with a maroon silk tie. After brief introductions, and a chat with Kenny, he turned to my mother and asked her to recount what she'd witnessed during Gabe's final appointment.

Her voice quivered. She broke down mid-sentence, tears flowing. I placed my hand on her shoulder and looked down, my own heart heavy.

The lawyer folded his hands and let out a sigh.

"I'm sorry for your loss," he said solemnly. "And for what you've been through."

He paused before continuing. "Before you proceed further, I need to be clear. Pursuing this case will be grueling. New York State malpractice laws are harsh. They leave little room for families to recover damages unless they are dependents; a spouse or children. It *will* feel unfair."

Though he acknowledged that malpractice had likely occurred based on the details and documentation he had so far, the lawyer wasn't sure his firm could take on the case. The potential financial return might not justify the investment it would require.

We shook hands, thanked him for his time, and watched the man stride away as he shifted focus to his next meeting.

A few minutes later, I sat in the waiting room, sipping water from a small paper cup. I looked at my mother, and something clicked into place.

"Mom," I said firmly, "we need to do this. What happened was wrong, and if there's even a *chance* at accountability, we have to try."

I crushed the cup in my hand.

"I don't care if we have to go to the worst-rated lawyer in the state. I just know this has to happen. I can't move forward until it does. This is the next task."

She nodded. Her voice was calm and certain. "Then let's do it."

We hugged Kenny goodbye in the lobby and stepped into the warm afternoon sun. People bustled by with iced coffees and office jackets slung over their arms, caught in the rhythm of a regular day.

"I think we need a change of scenery," Mom suggested.

We wandered down to the Seaport, where a trendy seltzer brand was hosting a pop-up. A young woman handed us cans from a dome-shaped cooler while a giant branded ping-pong table stood nearby.

Mom's eyes lit up.

My mother is a self-proclaimed "Idiot Savant of Games." Whatever the challenge, somehow, she wins. Ping-pong is Mom's favorite; her signature move a steady, unrelenting backhand that never changes *and* never misses. Eventually, she just outlasts you.

A tall, muscular guy stood at one end of the table. His partner stepped aside with a shrug of defeat.

"Mind if I play?" Mom asked.

He chuckled. "Sure, I'll go easy on you."

One minute in, he was darting left and right while Mom barely moved, calmly volleying her backhand over and over again.

I snapped a picture. Who else could walk out of a wrongful death consultation and immediately dominate a spontaneous ping-pong match? But that was our family ethos—finding slivers of light in dark places.

After Mom's victory, we walked along the water and stumbled across The Fulton, Chef Jean-Georges's new waterfront restaurant with a sweeping view of the Brooklyn Bridge. It was booked for weeks, but as we approached the host stand, a table for two magically opened up.

Soon we were seated beneath broad white umbrellas with nautical rope detailing, the East River shimmering beside us. We ordered spicy seafood pasta and a crisp white wine. In the center of the table stood a rose-gold lamp. As the sky darkened into dusk, I pulled its cord, and warm amber light bathed us in its glow.

Just as we were finishing, Mom's phone rang. It was the lawyer. His associates had reviewed the records, and he now felt *certain* we had a viable case.

A jolt of energy surged through me. *This is it,* I thought. *This is where I can put my focus. This is one more thing I can still do for Gabe.*

"Let's meet with a few more people," I said as she hung up.

Mom nodded, sipping her wine. "Okay. Although, today's experience might just be the legal world."

She peered at me over her glasses.

"So…we're really doing this?"

Before I could answer, the waiter arrived with dessert.

"Strawberry sundae, deconstructed!" he announced with theatrical flair.

Mom raised an eyebrow—ever the food purist. "Well, I didn't have high hopes for ice cream *deconstructed*. But this looks amazing."

On the table sat three bowls: one with scoops of fresh strawberry sorbet, another with miniature cookies and a glossy red sauce, and a third with a cloud of whipped cream. We fell into a contented silence, each of us building our own perfect spoonful.

"This is the kind of meal Gabe would've loved," I said at last.

Mom nodded, her voice soft. "I know he's here with us, Alee. I can feel it. That's why I'm able to keep going. We're going to keep having good experiences—the kind he and Dad would've wanted us to have. Because I know they want us to find a life we can enjoy."

She raised her glass to mine and smiled.

"A toast," she said. "To how bad-ass we were today."

SEPTEMBER, 2019: HUNTINGTON, NY

THE LONG FALL

*A*fter a full summer of moves, memorials, and heavy meetings, everyone drifted back into the patterns of their own days. While many people in our world were deeply sad, they still had their lives and responsibilities to return to. The leaves turned, and back at our house in Huntington, the hours of each day stretched on, unforgivingly long.

The lawsuit I had assumed would become my new focus was suddenly on hold. After the flurry of initial meetings and documentation, I learned it would be months before the next step.

I wasn't used to this kind of open time. For years I had kept a full schedule: work calls, family events, social gatherings, trips, workshops. The past year had added even more travel, along with caretaking. There was always something, always someone. And always, of course, there was a phone call or text thread with Gabe.

Now his phone lay silent in an empty kitchen drawer.

As the weeks passed, the hole my brother's absence left in my life felt like a tsunami—so big it swallowed everything else and left painful aftershocks of yearning in its wake.

Beyond missing Gabe, I was suddenly face to face with a new

kind of stillness. Life had been so vibrant, so mobile, for so long. I didn't know what it felt like to have an empty weekend, let alone an empty season.

Days were punctuated by solo walks around the block, distressing litigation emails, half-watched TV shows with Mom, or half-hearted attempts at cooking in the kitchen.

Until now, being busy had kept me safe. I had always been curious and creative, with plenty of interests. But purpose and productivity had also become my security system. I first began piling on activities when we were teenagers—and I never stopped.

The beginning of the cancer diagnoses in my family marked the start of my freshman year, and the final one came at the start of my senior year. Inside those years, I filled the space with activity: kick line, my first jobs, the school newspaper, a music industry internship, even a local TV panel. On afternoons off, if no one was home, I stayed late in the darkroom developing photos or tinkered with Photoshop in the computer lab.

I was called an old soul, a talented girl with a big future—and I liked that. I wanted to make my family proud, to keep up, to not miss my window of opportunity. Looking back, I can see it was also a strategy: a way to avoid feeling what was happening to us. The nights at the hospital, the uncertainty, the fear.

I found confidence when I was playing counselor to friends, sorting out troubles that seemed less overwhelming than my family's. I was chosen for 'Natural Helpers,' a peer support group formed by asking students to name the friend they turned to most. We were trained to become even *better* at this role, though most of us could have used support ourselves. Who was helping the Helpers?

After Dad died, I doubled down. I threw myself into new internships, a full-time job, the school newspaper, and life at my college party house. And then a health coach certification, energy healing attunements, and the pressure to secure at least ten clients before graduation, a prerequisite for the next training. All of it was good on its own, but together it was a *lot*. I had become someone who believed that free time meant failure—lost money, lost momentum, lost identity.

And even though I had dedicated much of my adult life to healing, both my own and others, I had never fully given myself the one ingredient I needed: space. At last, I was no longer in charge of deciding if I could take it. Like it or not, the space was here, vibrating with the painful echoes of everything I had tried to outrun.

My client contracts ended, and I knew I couldn't take on new ones. Letting go of people mid-process felt unsettling, but continuing would have been out of integrity, especially with my type of work.

For the first time in my adult life, I wasn't actively supporting clients clients or marketing to enroll them. I offered the occasional private session or newsletter, but that was it.

The idea of having a *real* practice again felt light-years away.

As destabilizing as the lack of work was, I was equally concerned about my health. I hadn't felt well in over a year, and everything intensified after Gabe's death.

I turned my attention to trying to fix my brain, hoping some doctor would tell me what was wrong, what I'd done wrong, and how to fix it all and get the old me back.

But, just like the lawsuit, that journey became another game of hurry-up-and-wait.

Doctors in New York said what the ones in LA had said: something was wrong, but mostly, I was heartbroken and in shock. What I needed most was time.

Still in my old mode, naturally that news led me to join an intense CrossFit-style gym called *ANIMAL INSTINCT!* Their logo was a pair of glowing, narrowed eyes above giant claw marks, as though an enormous paw had torn into the wall to write the words.

I punched, kicked, jumped and pushed—until my body started

swelling with even more inflammation. The animal of my body didn't need more stress to activate its instinct.

The only consistent ritual I managed that autumn was going to a new holistic detox center in town. Three times a week, I took the short drive into Huntington Village, the grief pressing against me like a titanium anvil.

The closer I got, the heavier it became, until it steamrolled me. Still, somehow, my pancake self walked and drove.

I finally understood what it meant to be "flattened by grief."

The woman at the front desk would greet me with a chipper voice that made me cringe. She'd hand me a towel and lead me to a small room with an infrared sauna. It was a big wooden box with a rainbow-colored lightbulb and a bench inside, heating to 150 degrees. I would undress, get in and sweat under the colored lights while reading books on grief: *On the Wild Edge of Sorrow*, *Bearing the Unbearable*, and *It's Okay to Not Be Okay*.

Next came the ionic foot-bath, a warm tub contraption to pull toxins from your feet. I would watch the swirling water turn murky earthen tones like I was watching fish in an aquarium, then check the laminated chart that explained what color represented what toxin.

Sometimes I left with the anvil slightly lighter. Sometimes not. And on the days it was just as heavy as when I started, there was nothing left to do but surrender to my broken heart.

I would curl up on the couch and scour through text messages with Gabe, my jaw set in a tight frown, reminiscing about how it had so recently been. Sometimes I tried to bypass my grief for a bit by scrolling through videos on YouTube, hoping a makeup tutorial would make me forget for a while, although I couldn't remember the last time I wore makeup.

I stopped engaging on social media.

Since 2007, I'd posted regularly: updates, stories, photos, celebrations and teachings. Now my page felt saturated with death and sadness. My social media had become the central hub for updates around Gabe's memorials along with many memorial posts my profile page was tagged in. In this grief portal, the creative spark or desire to be had vanished. I was in such severe pain that only privacy felt right. I didn't want to offer this experience as a bite-sized gem to be momentarily considered then scrolled past.

So I turned inward. I stopped writing and began to read, watch, and consume content instead. At first it brought relief, but soon it left me aching. Everyone else's life looked shinier, more exciting, more hopeful than anything I could imagine for myself again. Even those who had behaved selfishly during this time now appeared noble online, with well-timed captions and filtered compassion.

Scrolling through the videos and photos offered distraction while stirring waves of comparison and grief. My broken heart whispered that the world was moving on, thriving even, while I remained left behind and alone. The one person I wanted to unpack this with was gone forever. It felt like a punishment.

Why hadn't our good efforts been enough for him to stay? All of these healthcare practitioners, both mainstream and holistic, had so confidently claimed to know what was wrong with Gabe. And they were all wrong. *No one* had caught the true issue in time. My brother had been a voice of integrity in this industry, someone so many relied on in their own healing—and it had not mattered in the end. I lost faith in the world that Gabe and I had immersed ourselves in since college.

I knew I wouldn't ultimately lose my entire life philosophy or spiritual understanding to this tragedy; those very foundations had carried me this far. I still stayed connected to a few trusted teachers and practices, but I wasn't open to anything new.

It was time for a major shift. For now, *any* practice or energy I worked with would have to be big enough to hold my rejection of it. ***Everything* was going into the fire**, and one day I'd see what had made it through.

I needed support, but not a coach. I didn't want to be some-one's testimonial, or guided through a marketing funnel. Even the best version of that model assumes stability and function—both of which I had in short supply. I couldn't set any more goals or take on any more accountability than I already had.

It was time to sit with someone who understood grief clinically. Someone with no agenda. Someone who could meet me in the dark without insisting I turn on the light.

For the first time in my life, I couldn't promise I wanted to be anyone's "success story," not even my own. I couldn't promise anything—except that I wanted to survive.

OCTOBER 2019 HUNTINGTON, NY

THE THERAPIST

"*H*as any of this trauma caused you to pull out your hair or pick at your skin?" Dr. Feldman asked, her blue eyes wide. "Because really, *that's* my specialty."

I was sitting across from my first attempt at finding a therapist through insurance. She wore an elegant tan suit and seemed completely overwhelmed by my story, especially once it was confirmed that it did not, in fact, include trichotillomania.

The next therapist required a harrowing drive across parkways, a journey that immediately triggered memories of the hellish Florida road trip. I finally arrived at what turned out to be an upscale retirement village. A smiling older woman with bright red hair that matched her lipstick answered the door. We walked past her elderly husband watching TV in the living room beside her office, which was filled with family photos and an old-school fax machine.

I sat across from her, still shaking from the drive, and felt like I was visiting someone's grandparents. I realized I'd need therapy *after* therapy just to recover from the commute.

I tried again, this time booking an appointment with someone whose office was just a few minutes from home. Once it was scheduled, I googled her name and found over 75 reviews—all echoing the same alarming observation.

> "Has snoozed her way through every session."

> "She is half-asleep every time I've met with her."

> "You must clap at the end of every appointment to wake her up. Still, it's nice to have someone to sit with while I talk."

I cancelled our meeting, but didn't have the energy to suggest she look into a sleep study.

Giving the insurance list one more shot, I clicked on the final Psychology Today profile for a therapist in my town. From Karin's photo, she looked to be in her late 40s, with a highlighted brown bob, a wide smile, and eclectic beaded jewelry. I felt a flicker of cautious hope.

Karin's office was in a historic Victorian house just a few minutes from where I lived. I parked behind the building and entered the first floor, which was home to the local political head-quarters. It was filled with campaign posters and young staffers speaking loudly into phones. But just one floor up, the energy was completely different.

I climbed the narrow steps and knocked on Karin's door, entering a small, cozy room with Himalayan salt lamps and photographs from her travels. From the moment we met, she never seemed overwhelmed, just curious and compassionate. I also noticed something else—for once, I wasn't urgently spilling my guts.

There was no compulsion to share the entire story and all the self-diagnosed problems as I saw it, or to disassociate with the painful details, my eyes focused on her reaction, until I couldn't feel the story I spoke of was even *mine.*

At our first session, I stayed with the most important parts: that my brother had died suddenly, and I was back living with my mom while we figured it all out. Karin nodded, then calmly shared her first reflection.

"This is going to take some time to really unravel," she said gently. "There's a lot going on here. One small piece after another. We don't have to rush."

I couldn't remember the last time I had sought support without a major goal, tight timeline, or sizable investment.

I breathed in this new idea and thought back to something Mom had said on a heavy day, when the invisible anvil on my chest felt unbearable:

"This isn't something you'll move on from in a few months," she told me. "Gabe was your person. It's going to take years."

It felt both true and terrifying.

The idea of ever finding my way again after such a loss seemed impossible. And yet I also felt pressure to keep going, not just for me, but for him. His life had been cut short at the cusp of so many things.

"I can't fall apart for too long," I told a friend, mere weeks after it happened. "It would be unfair to him and everything he built. Gabe wasn't finished, and I have to continue on for him."

I felt a duty to represent my brother, to carry forward his vision as I understood it. To prove that the path of healing we had chosen back in college wasn't in vain. And after years of devoted work in coaching, ceremonies, and practices, after countless hours of showing up for my own healing, *shouldn't* I be able to hold it together at least a little better than the average bear?

But slowly, the surrender began.

I began to soften into the reality of how long this would take. I gave myself permission to step back from the people I had once engaged with out of obligation to my brother. I stopped trying to prove myself to those I didn't feel safe enough to fall apart with.

And I booked two sessions a week with Karin.

As our work continued, the bigger picture began to emerge. Yes, of course this grief was about Gabe. But it was also about everything that came before it: years of holding, years of caregiving, years of trying to heal and inspire instead of feeling where I was hurt or disappointed.

I once again remembered being 23 and having panic attacks between my two graduations. The unspoken belief that *it was all on me.*

I also began to see just how much my relationship with Mom had been shaped by this. For years we had been at an impasse, our recovery styles pulling us in opposite directions. I needed to talk through everything; she preferred to keep things close. I wanted a life untethered from the story I had grown up with, while she still expected me to return whenever the family story called. Both of us were overrun with tending to others.

In therapy, my experiences were validated and my trauma responses named. My spirituality and supernatural encounters were not dismissed or pathologized but received with respect.

There were no action items, no upsells, no pressure.

This support, which felt groundbreaking, was also covered by insurance. After a couple of months, I showed up with guilt.

"Not everything I've tried has been helpful. Some things even harmed more than they helped. I paid thousands. Now you're my lifeline in Huntington...and I barely pay a thing."

Karin smiled.

"Well, your insurance is paying me what I ask," she said. "But I think it was meant to be this way. Not paying me directly is especially healing for you. It's time to divest from transactional ways of being."

I began to see how unyielding I'd been with myself, pouring my budget into nonstop coaching, classes, and events. Sure, there was also fun to be had, but I had skipped too many milestones with friends outside that world, just to make the next training. And many of the workshop people I had prioritized? Not really present now. What if what I really needed was simply time with the friends who could be—and the space to rest?

I was finally experiencing the unavoidable collapse after years of overriding my body's call for down-time . When the big push of traumas came this year, my system was already on the edge.

Now it was time to unwind it all.

Gently and one string at a time.

Karin reminded me this wasn't just grief work. It was a deprogramming from the cult of relentless self-optimization. From this space, I began to untangle from the idea that these losses had happened because we had done something wrong—or could have been prevented if we had only done it right.

I loosened my grip on the belief that *everything* could be solved, that everyone, including me, could be fixed if I just tried hard enough or took enough accountability.

I had to begin to trust the design of life, even when it unfolded far beyond my preferences. Some things could not be changed. It was a revelation, though it didn't take the pain away.

The holidays were hard; it felt like I spent most of the season managing other people's reactions to our first year without Bubbie and Gabe instead of tending to my own. I was still afraid the best years were over, even as I could see some cracks more clearly. My heart was broken, yet something small had begun to shift—a new way was emerging.

Part of that way came from understanding my limitations. In this very early stage of recovery, I simply wasn't who I remembered, and I had to acknowledge the raw truth of what this process really required.

When I tried to socialize in the ways I remembered as bringing joy, like visiting friends in other cities, the reality quickly set in. I could barely handle the crowds, the noise, the late nights, or the lack of privacy to grieve. I didn't know how to ask for things I had never needed before. And feeling disconnected from my professional identity left me believing that everyone else's schedule mattered more than mine.

So instead of honoring my current reality, I tried to appear more together than I was: overly generous and ambitious with plans. I'd show up cheerfully with gifts for my friends' kids, rushing around the city to accommodate their lives. After a few days of this, I would collapse into tears and anxiety that lingered well into the next week. In this time of PTSD, my body and mind were fragile, ready to spiral out from the slightest extra demand.

The truth was that I had to take in the nutrient of friendship, vital as it was, in small doses. Once that became clear, a handful of friends in New York became part of a new season—just enough connection to remind me I still had deep roots here, even while I felt unmoored.

There were the hometown friends who, with a walk in the park or over a glass of wine, reminded me I was still in the living world —with people who had truly loved my family and wanted me to feel part of their own. Celeste's son, Britt, had married my childhood friend Carolyn, and it was comforting to have a family nearby with whom I shared many memories, often tinged with humor in the retelling of them.

Some of the friendships that had carried me through earlier seasons of life now had space to grow close again; not just through shared history, but from the present moment.

Susan and I had known each other since junior high and stayed close through college, but as adults our lives had taken different paths across the country, and we didn't get to connect in person often. Now, suddenly back in the same place, there was room for our old closeness to return, and for us to notice the parallels in our lives and share the present together.

When I could make the trip into the city, she welcomed me with warmth: a candle lit, music playing, a chalkboard by the door that read *Welcome, Alee!*—and always with a beautiful charcuterie platter. Sometimes we watched movies and caught up with another childhood friend, Christina; other times I simply collapsed into the big couch that had been made up with plush blankets and pillows for me. Just being there was enough.

Sarah, one of my closest friends from college, was now a renowned tarot reader and medium in Manhattan. We loved to cackle like the witches we are—whether it was over absurd twenty-something memories, or the uncanny ways we saw the world alike. She pulled cards when I asked, and simply listened when the future felt too heavy to contemplate. We kept a regular coffee ritual, even when it was nothing more than a cup over the phone.

I also inherited new connections. Arul, who had once run a wellness center in the city with Gabe, became part of my inner circle, along with her kids. My brother had been close with all of them, and Mom and I found our own family bond with theirs as well. They loved sharing stories of Gabe as the NYC local he had been with them—playing basketball with her son, or as the audience for her daughter's song-and-dance performances. Later, Arul and I would collaborate on healing projects of our own.

These threads gently steadied me in the midst of upheaval. A few hours with friends, or the occasional apartment overnight, was enough to remind me what it felt like to belong. And then they returned to their lives, and I went back to my own daily reality. Nothing could change the place I was in: dense with sorrow, recovery still far off, a life upended. It was simply how things were.

I wrote in my community newsletter that fall,

I have found it is imperative to get comfortable with suffering.
To know it comes for all of us at different times in life.
To know it is not a punishment—but in fact
a guaranteed part of the awakened human experience,
Just as pleasure is.

JANUARY, 2020: HUNTINGTON, NY

THE FIRST BIRTHDAY

We were standing in a wide circle around the tree, bracing against the bitter cold with hats and scarves, and in my case, a face mask. I wasn't sure if the bug I had picked up from a visiting friend was the new illness called coronavirus.

Heckscher Park was just a few minutes from our family home. It was over 100 years old, filled with flowers and trees, a playground, an art museum, and an outdoor bandshell. This had been the scene of Gabe's infamous performance as one half of *The Blues Brothers* during a town festival. No nine-year-old had ever looked more like a weathered John Belushi, and the crowd roared.

We spent our childhood here, flinging off the swings into the sandbox while Bubbie watched nervously from the side. We'd tear through the jungle gym and attend the summer arts camp inside the museum.

The best part of Heckscher was the walking path that looped around the pond, where ducks and swans glided across the surface and turtles sunbathed on floating branches in every season but winter.

As an adult, the park had become Gabe's favorite place to practice Qigong in warmer months, standing barefoot by the trees. The week before he died, he texted me a picture of himself in this exact spot—just before heading back to Miami.

Now we were here again. It was Gabe's 39th birthday, the first since he had died.

We honored him the way we knew how: with a ceremony that gave way to a crowded table and a communal meal. We hadn't yet brought my brother's ashes anywhere, but on his birthday, in front of his favorite tree at Heckscher, it felt like the right place to begin.

Several of his closest local friends had taken the day off to join us in the cold, along with a few family members. James and Sean were there, plus James' mom, Susan, a sharp-witted redhead with a crackling sense of humor who could keep up with every playful jab from the guys.

We stood in a circle, each person sharing a favorite Gabe memory before scattering ashes at the base of the tree.

It was Susan's turn. Tears welled in her eyes.

"Some of my happiest memories are of all the boys having big sleepovers in the basement and—"

In my peripheral vision, I saw something speeding across the lawn.

A blur.

I squinted. It was a large man in a full navy windbreaker set, zooming toward us on an electric scooter. One of his legs was in a cast, propped horizontally on a shelf built into the ride.

I wasn't sure he would stop. But at the last second, he screeched to a halt, no more than two inches from Susan, peering over her shoulder. Everyone saw him now.

"I was there, too," he breathed, looking meaningfully into Susan's eyes.

"You... you were at the sleepover?" she asked, her voice shaky as she tried to recall if she had ever made French toast in the 90s for this now-grown man.

Then he looked around at all of us and repeated it, more firmly.

"*I was there, **too**.*"

I turned and suddenly saw it: just beyond Gabe's tree stood a metal gauntlet sculpture, welded from steel taken from the Twin Towers. Beside it was a small reflection fountain, inscribed with names.

We weren't only in my brother's place of Zen. We were standing steps from the park's September 11th memorial.

That's where he had been. He thought we were gathering for a survivors' support group.

"Oh God," I said quickly. "Sir, I'm so sorry, but this isn't for 9/11—it's a memorial for someone else."

He gave us a casual shrug. "Oh, gotcha," he said breezily, like it was a mix-up at the deli. Then he U-turned his scooter around Susan, gunned it back to top speed, and zipped across the lawn, out the exit, and off to his next adventure.

We stood in stunned silence for a beat. Then Mom started to giggle. Everyone followed.

It was exactly the kind of thing Dad or Gabe would have told us about: a surreal encounter, a funny character, a new catch-phrase for the archives. Dark humor delivered with just the right amount of *Curb Your Enthusiasm* guilt.

That night, I lay in bed after the long day. We had included all of Gabe's favorite things: a good meal, inside jokes, ceremony. The only thing missing was the Super Bowl. He had always loved when it fell on his birthday.

And most of all, of course, we missed Gabe himself.

Just then, a photo popped up on my phone's memory feature. It was from the Venice Canals, taken just before his 38th birthday, his last one alive. Gabe was beaming at the camera, and I was laughing with my eyes closed.

During the holidays, all the canals in Venice are decorated with lights and themed bridges. We had wandered onto one called The

Wishing Bridge, strung with tiny lights and baskets holding paper tags and pens for visitors to write their wishes.

As Aquarian siblings, his birthday in late January and mine two weeks later in February, we wrote our birthday wishes to hang there together.

I remembered watching as Gabe thoughtfully filled his tag with multiple dreams and hopes for the year, then carefully tied it back onto the bridge, his handwriting looping across the paper.

So many goals, so many plans. He had been so sure of where he was headed. The image stayed with me.

Until then, I had believed that if someone no longer had dreams or direction, it might mean their time was almost up. That maybe the absence of momentum was some kind of omen.

But it turns out you can still be writing your grandest wishes on a wishing bridge right before everything disappears.

FEBRUARY, 2020: BROOKLYN, NY

THE MUSHROOM ODYSSEY

" Take everything off, lie down, and I'll be right back in."

I hobbled into a room shrouded in tapestries and fairy lights and tried to take off my clothes while balancing on one leg. This is *not* what I expected when I had booked myself an overnight at a fancy hotel. The booking in itself had been quite an endeavor; reserving a nice room or a dinner out when your birthday is on Valentine's Day keeps the competition tight.

This was my first birthday without Gabe and without my old life. Previously, I had always loved throwing a big "V-Day/B-Day" gathering. But now acknowledging my birthday felt like a tender tension- the pull between craving support while also wishing to slip through unseen.

I was desperate for the promise of a new year, while being terrified for any more time to pass. After this birthday I would no longer be the same age I had been when Gabe was still alive. This weekend began the march into the rest of my life and all the future birthdays where my brother would be missing.

It felt like when I left being 35, I would officially leave Gabe.

I thought back to my 34th birthday, the last one where I had really felt good. I was still living in California then, and a dozen or so friends had joined me for a hike through a mountainous vineyard along the Malibu coast — a place that, in true West coast fashion, also housed a variety of exotic, trained animal performers, retired from years of filming Hollywood movies, now hand-fed pellets by tipsy hikers.

That's L.A. for you.

We joyfully strolled the grounds under warm sunshine, stopping by the sprawling enclosure of a celebrity giraffe named Stanley. He was famous for his many television and film roles — "whenever and wherever a live giraffe was required." Now, Stanley's only job was to pose for photo ops while eating snacks.

Our guide handed me a large piece of lettuce and instructed me to hold one end in my mouth. As I did, Stanley— right on cue — came galloping toward me, gingerly extending his enormous black tongue to wrap around the other half of the leaf and pull it into his gummy mouth.

Shrieking with laughter, my friends snapped the moment: an homage to the Lady and the Tramp spaghetti scene, starring me, Stanley and a lettuce leaf.

Afterwards, we gathered at a large wooden table surrounded by lush vineyards for an eight-flight wine tasting. Before every tasting new glass, someone at the table would offer a toast of gratitude, each one more elaborate and theatrical than the last. We swirled, sniffed, and sipped, laughing and cheering between rounds.

When I returned from the bathroom after the tasting, my friend Ryan placed a real flower crown made of red roses and daisies on my head.

"There's a lady at a table making them. You needed a birthday crown," he said, giving me a hug.

I hugged him back, my heart full, and we all drifted toward a live band playing nearby in front of a large sign that said,

The Doctors Are Out!

It was a group of retired plastic surgeons wearing scrubs and playing Carlos Santana covers.

That's L.A. for you.

We danced to *Black Magic Woman*, our cheeks flushed with fresh air, red Zinfandel, and joy.

If only we could go back. But nothing reminds you that time only moves forward quite like a birthday.

This weekend would be an attempt at honoring the passage of time without asking for too much from anyone, including myself. I wasn't sure how to ask others to celebrate what didn't feel much like a celebration, or to make their Valentine's Day about me.

Before this, I had always loved filling my apartment with heart-shaped treats, pink and red decorations, good music, and a circle of friends soon to be connected. Sometimes I had a boyfriend, sometimes I didn't, but romance was always in the air. It had always been a time to celebrate the gift of my life.

But now I was running on fumes, unsure how a heart this broken could ever open to falling in love again, and wondering if life was even worth celebrating—or if *I* was, when it felt like I had nothing left to give.

In therapy I had begun unwinding a deeper story hidden underneath my ideas about friendship. Somewhere along the way, I had created an unspoken rule: to have people around for my special day, there *had* to be something offered in exchange.

No wonder, then, that once there was nothing fun left to give, some of those connections began to dissolve. They had been built on a premise I could no longer sustain.

Even with all the inner conflict, my desperate desire to take a proper bath finally got me out of my head and onto a train towards the hotel.

I'd settled on a modern hotel in Long Island City; a renovated factory with cement floors but sweeping skyline views and, most importantly, a large soaking tub. I missed my once-daily salt baths and ocean swims now that I only had a shower. Once the room was secured, I hit up a LUSH store, treating myself to a variety of bath bombs and bubbles, hoping one night of soaking could replace many months without it.

I got to the hotel and burst in the door, threw down my heavy bag, and laid across the crisp white sheets of the hotel bed. For a minute I was quiet, breathing in the private luxury in with deep breaths. Then I flipped on the TV and rested my head on a pillow as an old episode of *Law and Order SVU* filled the screen.

When I began to unpack, I decided to have dinner at the hotel restaurant before submerging myself in a hot cocktail of bath products. *The perfect night.* But that's when my phone buzzed. It was Chelsea, a girl who worked at the detox store in Huntington.

> Hey, are you in NYC tonight? He said no problem, you can come over to pick it up!

She had mentioned a few weeks earlier that she might know a connection to an herbalist in the city who could help me start micro-dosing psilocybin. This had been recommended to me to help treat the PTSD that sent me into those week-long spirals when I overexerted myself.

Now, with an address and an invite to meet Chelsea over there at 9 p.m., there was a decision to make. I didn't *feel* like leaving the cocoon of the hotel, but what of this was my only chance to get something that could really help?

I put the luxury bath plans on hold and with a little time to spare, ordered a salad and pizza at the restaurant, savoring every bite.

One hour later, my cab driver let me out onto a funky street deep in Brooklyn, where hipsters braced the snow flurries in tight leather jackets and even tighter jeans, off to the next bar or house party. I knocked on the door, and Chelsea answered with a big smile on her face.

"Welcome!" she said with a hug. "He's just finishing with a patient."

This was a home office, and not like one I had been to recently. Posters of Chinese herbs hung neatly next to psychedelic art and underground rave flyers. We sat on a linen couch with a glossy wooden floor. Another man with neon orange hair and muscles the size of kegs came through the door dressed in gym clothes. He held up two slightly greasy paper bags and looked up at Chelsea and I with a grin.

"I just had such an intense workout and then got sooo many tacos. I'm about to go HAM!," he announced.

"The roommate," she explained as he walked past us and into the kitchen.

Finally, at half past 9, the acupuncturist known as Dr. Lynx entered. He was tall and fit, with big green eyes and long bleached dreaded hair shaved on both sides, almost like a warrior mohawk. Lynx was wearing loose hemp pants and a slim fitting faux fur jacket.

"Hey, welcome!" he said with a smile as he bounded around the room. "Sorry, this last appointment is really running late. How about you settle in with some coca leaf power? It's what I use to keep myself going on these longer session days."

Dr. Lynx had a long wooden bookshelf lined with glass jars and selected one filled with a dark powder. He pinched off a bit and placed it in the inside of his cheek, and then offered me a small spoonful and told me to do the same.

"Just let it dissolve there. This is what the farmers in South America do to stay focused on the fields! Hang out and I'll be back soon."

I placed the coca leaf powder on the inside of my cheek. It tasted bitter, earthy, tangy, and strings of grit started to slide down my throat. I thought back to my lovely hotel room bathtub, but quickly let the image go. I *needed* to get these mushrooms—what if they could help my brain? I hoped he was right that the powder would not do anything but make me feel a little more energized.

I sat for another 20 minutes with Chelsea when I started to feel a tingling in my right ankle. I looked down and it was swelling before my eyes, like Veruca Salt in *Charlie and The Chocolate Factory* when she turns into a blueberry. Then the deep ache set in.

"Holy shit, what's happening?!" I yelped.

I realized this was the ankle I had sprained two months earlier. As far as I knew, it had healed well enough. I was back to exercising and walking on it, even in the cute platform boots I had worn over here.

Lynx was still in his other session. I grabbed my phone and googled more about coca leaf powder, looking for side effects. What I found was that energetically, coca leaf was considered a heart medicine. It connected one to the truth of the matter.

I sat with that idea, trying not to freak out. Maybe my ankle hadn't fully healed. Or maybe I hadn't learned how to sit with myself, and the lesson wasn't over. I thought back to when the injury first happened. It was from falling in a *Zumba class*, of all things. Right after, I'd gotten into a screaming match with Mom, more about our grief over the upcoming holidays than anything else.

After the fight I was on the phone with the manager of a telesummit company, ankle elevated on a pillow, to discuss launching a new program. There I was: attempting to sell healing facilitation to hundreds of people while navigating life back in my hometown, the beginnings of the lawsuit, and my first holiday season without Gabe and Bubbie.

Looking back, it was absurd to try and launch something new in that moment. But at the time, I was pushing myself, terrified I had lost my business and my relevance as a healer along with everything else.

That night, I talked to Matt, a friend from the telesummit circuit. We had first met five years earlier, when we were both chosen to launch energy healing programs on the same show, and had quickly become allies.

Matt was an interesting mix: a grounded father and husband, a devoted yogi, and a former contractor turned *powerful* light-language channel and healer. Matt and his wife, Marie, a renowned yoga teacher, ran sold-out retreats around the world. He once told me their kids explained his job to a friend's parents by saying, *"My dad says gobbledy-gook for a living!"* which made us both laugh.

"How'd the meeting go?" he asked in his cheerful New Zealand accent.

I answered tightly, trying to convince myself more than him.

"I mean, I want to do it. I feel like it's time to move forward, but my ankle hurts and my mom is driving me crazy today..." I trailed off, afraid the knot in my throat would turn into tears if I kept talking.

"Alee," he said gently, "it's not time to move forward with this. You're just getting started in your *own* process. The telesummit doesn't need you to get back to work. *You* need you—to drop in, release the pressure, and take care of yourself. It's time to begin your own healing. I'd reckon that's what your ankle is telling you. Just sit down and *be* with yourself."

I cancelled the launch and spent the next few weeks trying, although with a strong helping of distraction. I read books and Reddit threads on anything I could think of and rewatched Season Four of *Game of Thrones*. I iced my ankle and tried not worry that everything would slip away but the fear was too great. Besides that, the stubborn weight gain was still there, and I was just as afraid of gaining even more without keeping up my regular workouts.

So I got back to it.

I had thought it had been enough time to heal the sprain, but now it seemed like the coca leaf powder had made a beeline for the recent injury. No, my body wasn't healed. I hadn't spent enough time giving it space to recover. And no, I wasn't ready or even *wanting* to be gallivanting around town, mushrooms or not. I thought of my long-awaited hotel room, now sitting empty. It was clear that I still didn't have my own permission to relax, if I could be on a mission of some sort.

At this point, Dr. Lynx was finally ready. He walked out to the couch, and his eyes widened when he saw my leg propped up.

"After the coca leaf powder, my ankle sent a message," I said.

And that's how I found myself on a treatment table framed in rave lights, my body covered in acupuncture needles like a porcupine, with Chelsea doing Reiki above me.

My ankle was unyielding; it stayed so sore and swollen I couldn't even step on it. Lynx tried every acupuncture protocol he knew, but eventually it was time to admit defeat. I hobbled off the table, pulled my clothes back on, and sank down on the couch. He and Chelsea sat with me, their faces kind and concerned.

"If coca leaf brings attention to the truth, then I guess the truth is that it's hard to let new people in right now." A tear rolled down my cheek. "I really appreciate how much you both are trying," I added. "Receiving help, after losing confidence in myself, feels very...*intense.*"

I told them a little more of the story, and they responded with compassion. I gave them both hugs, paid Dr. Lynx, and called a cab.

"Oh! The mushrooms!" he said brightly.

Right. The mushrooms. I turned, expecting vitamin-like capsules. Instead, he handed me a few literal dried magic mushrooms.

"You can take a little nibble of the cap or the stem each day and see how you do," he suggested.

I sighed. I knew he meant well, but the intense vigilance guarding my system needed something more measured and regulated than that.

"Thanks, but I think I'm good for now," I said.

I hobbled barefoot down the icy cement stoop and into the cab, then up the steps to the hotel lobby, into the elevator, and finally—blessedly—back into the room.

It was after midnight. I had missed most of my evening at the hotel, but I could still ring in the first hour of my 36th year as planned. I turned on the faucet and let the large clawfoot tub fill with hot water, then tossed my favorite LUSH bath bomb in—a bright blue ball filled with seaweed, mineral salt, and citrus oil. It fizzed and snapped on the top of the steamy water, turning it a shimmering cobalt. I gently lowered myself in and closed my eyes.

The next night, I met friends for dinner at an Italian restaurant in the East Village called Crispo. I limped thought the door, putting as much weight as possible on my left foot as I was led through the restaurant. A wave of joy rolled through me when I saw where we would be seated: a big table in front of a wood-burning oven and fireplace. Everyone else was already there, celebrating the good fortune of our location and ordering a bottle of wine.

I sat down and gave out little gifts: heart-shaped tea lights and chocolates, eye masks, and grade-school valentine cards. I'd enjoyed putting a little something together, to still have something to give in the name of love and friendship.

Then came the family-style platters of food. There was roasted bone marrow with fresh herbs and grilled bread, homemade pasta in a ragu, and broccoli rabe, steamed to an emerald green. We enjoyed the warm and and intimate connection that happens when a group of people share really great food. I smiled thinking of last year and my final dinner with Gabe and Mom, also rustic Italian family-style.

Tears suddenly blurred my vision, and I rubbed my eyes before looking around the table—love and friendship gathered in one place. People from my past, people who knew my brother, people who belonged to this moment: James and his wife Courtney; Jess, my brother's junior-prom date and a close friend to us both; Neenah, also recently returned to Long Island after years away; and Susan, Christina, and Dylan. The throbbing in my ankle felt further away.

Not everyone who had been an integral part of prior celebrations could be there. Not everyone who I had felt so close to until recently had even called. It was a different type of birthday dinner than the past, but it was the *right* one. These were the friends who could show up, who were available to get to this restaurant on a cold winter's night in New York City.

These were the ones who could stomach my grief, which came with the meal like a wine pairing, and still enjoy my company. Any ideas I'd carried about who *should* or *would* be in my life during this devastating season had to be released as I stepped into a new year. It was time to put my heartfelt gratitude on the community that was with me now.

JUNE, 2020: HUNTINGTON, NY

THE COVID BEACH CLUB

*M*om splashed her feet and took a sip of her newest cocktail recipe, now known as *The Fab Flamingo*: tequila, grapefruit, and limeade, topped with a tiny pink umbrella.

The first Covid Summer had begun. The promise of the world reopening in time for beaches, camps, or summer parties had proven to be a false alarm. Wedding season was also on ice—now only announced as a cautionary tale, morbidly detailing whose elderly relatives had died after the reception.

So we would be staying put here in Huntington, and Mom had made the decision that it was time to turn our backyard into the country club that never was. Currently, she was cooling off in the large inflatable pool I had driven to three different Targets to score, filled with water from the garden hose.

Plastic pink flamingos sunned themselves to her right and to the left was the foosball table from Gabe's thirteen birthday, gathering dust in the basement no more. Above her, a large tiki-style umbrella shaded a palm-printed outdoor rug spread over the wooden deck. A small speaker rotated through songs from Bonnie Raitt, James Taylor, and The Beatles.

"Who needs a beach club?" she said as she looked over at me and splashed her feet again. "I feel like I'm on the Riviera!"

At the bottom of the deck, through the window of what had been Bubbie's mother-in-law apartment when I was growing up, I watched Mom's tenant—and my current arch-nemesis—Enid, staring into a cosmetic mirror with her hair in rollers, drawing on dark arched eyebrows.

Her slight body was dwarfed by her beloved cat, Richie, an *enormous* tabby with glowing green eyes, who seemed bigger than she was. Enid noticed me watching through the blinds, gave a curt nod and polite smile, and shut the curtain. She had been on good behavior since our climactic run-in last week.

We hadn't interacted much since she moved into the unit. I'd been living away for years; Bubbie had moved to a nearby retirement village in my late teens, and some time after my dad passed, Mom began renting the apartment to a few tenants, ending with Enid. When I visited, it always felt strange that what had once been Bubbie's warm, cozy space now housed this eccentric woman and her cat. But I was rarely back long enough to dwell on it. She kept to herself, preferring to stay inside with Richie.

After Gabe died, it was like a switch flipped.

The week of his funeral, as I was printing memorial photos at Kinko's, she left long and winding voicemails to tell me she had called the police, the fire department, and "the town" about us—for reasons unknown.

"She's never been like this, but who knows? I guess she's getting wacky, she's had a hard life," Mom surmised.

This didn't bother her as it did me; she had bigger fish to fry. But the injustice of this bad behavior taking place simultaneously with Gabe's loss, and the indignity of this being the shoddy welcome back home felt like a problem I had to solve.

First, I tried kindness. I took out her garbage and brought in her groceries, including the industrial-sized bags of kitty litter.

"Hello, Enid! How are you?" I would ask pleasantly, as I hoisted another bag from the front porch into what had been Bubbie's kitchen. I would talk to her about psychology, and she would tell me about her therapist's newest suggestions.

But every few weeks, like a sudden storm, her mood would darken, her grievances would come raining down, and she would shriek in a high-pitched tone. We had contacted her local family, who made it clear they considered us her de facto caretakers. It was obvious it was time for Enid to move on. But how—and *when* —in the midst of a pandemic, remained an open question.

Last week had been the breaking point. She was furious about something indistinct and had, once again, fixated on Mom as her "evil landlord." I walked downstairs. Enid had opened the small door from her apartment into our den and was yelling.

That door had once been the portal into Narnia when I was little: a little escape for all of us, where happy little Bubbie toasted bagels and brewed coffee, the pleasant buzz of talk radio in the background. Where she was always ready to greet her grandchildren and their friends with a big smile and a glass of fresh orange juice.

Now I watched this small woman, decidedly not like Bubbie, face contorted with anger, and behind her, as always, Richie, his fluffy tail flicking to the beat of her shouted words.

"The problem is you're a liar!" she shrieked. "And everyone knows it!"

Mom answered evenly, "Okay, that's enough."

"No, no, it's true. Even your own son knew it!" Enid sputtered, gathering steam. "He was very nice. And we used to have very pleasant conversations, ones in which we discussed your *lying*!"

For a moment, I almost laughed picturing Gabe and Enid on the porch, sipping iced tea and gossiping. But when she continued, "Gabe would always say—" the amusement burned off like dry grass.

A fierce instinct surged through me. The role of family protector, passed to me from my brother, who had taken it from Dad. I'd stepped into it when we faced lawyers, negotiated with his business partners, or fended off contractors trying to up-charge once they saw it was a female homeowner. And now, in front of Enid, as she fabricated a story about my brother.

I stepped in front of Mom, inches from her face.

"Stop saying my brother's name," I said, the force rising in me like a wave I couldn't hold back. "How dare you say that to my mother when she is grieving her son. How dare you create chaos here during this sad time, for reasons that have nothing to do with us!"

Enid's eyes widened, and she went silent. The nice daughter who carried her groceries had finally been pushed too far.

Later that day she tearfully apologized to Mom. I watched from the porch as Mom watered plants and spoke in a calm tone.

"Apology accepted. I know you're having a hard time. But we can't have this going on anymore."

From then on, Lady E was as meek as a mouse around me.

"I think you scared some sense into her," Mom said. "She told me to apologize to you, too."

I went back to carrying packages and exchanging polite greetings, but the precedent was set. I wondered if anyone had ever been afraid of me before; jolted by my fury and the power it hinted at.

Very few people had ever seen me truly angry. Most of my life had been spent making others comfortable. Kindness, insight, and accessibility had been my currency. But now, in this strange new season, I was learning to be firm and fierce. Maybe it wasn't the worst thing if someone disliked me.

The mentally questionable cat lady in Bubbie's old apartment wasn't the most impressive attempt at letting my anger set the boundary, but it had worked.

A few of Mom's close friends—our COVID bubble—would come by to sit by the inflatable pool and drink Fab Flamingos under the tiki umbrella. These women had known me since I was born, and welcomed me back with open arms.

Even so, it wasn't easy to be seventy-ish in the pandemic. For many of them, Summer 2020 was supposed to be their moment: retirements celebrated, vacations enjoyed, grandkids hugged.

Now everything was on pause.

By late June, times stretched endlessly ahead. Unlike the previous summer, when I'd come home from Miami at the very start of it all, there *truly* seemed to be no end in sight. My thoughts spun.

What if I was paused here for years? What if all the good times of my life were already over, as it still felt after Gabe? And why *should* I expect more, when the best person I'd ever known had been cut off at 38?

What if the rest of my existence played out in a viral apocalypse, living in my childhood bedroom in a state of perpetual yearning, nostalgia, and regret? What if my unhinged run-ins with Enid were the peak of my in-person social life for years to come? It all felt dangerously close to possible.

One silver lining was getting to know Mom differently, as both a person and a friend. By this point, we had been working together as a team for more than a year. With all this space to spend together, I could more fully appreciate her sense of humor and her impulse to find something celebratory in every season—even this one.

Growing up, our house was the place for parties. After the first day of school, everyone wanted to come over, where Mom's treat platter waited on the table, flanked by shiny mylar balloons with her signature back-to-school phrase written in bubble letters with a Sharpie:

"IT'S COOL TO LIKE SCHOOL!"

But alongside the celebrations, given everything else that was happening, there was also intensity, stress, and conflict. For most of the last fifteen years, I had been leaving the conversation, the room, or the house as quickly as possible. Now I was back in a holding pattern, reconnecting with her personality without the tension *or* the possibility of getting away.

It wasn't easy. Most of my friends and peers were Covid-bubbling with partners, siblings, same-age neighbors. It amplified how much I felt like I had nobody left but my mother. I was glad we were getting along, but I didn't fully know how to meet her ability to appreciate our circumstances.

Sometimes it felt as if my fifteen years away from Huntington hadn't happened at all. It was a season when everyone's life seemed frozen, like insects suspended in amber. For me, the pause came *just* as I had let everything go to return home, grieve, and reconcile.

Had all my travels, explorations, and hard-won growth simply led me back here?

Through the lens of grief, I found myself wishing I had chosen differently. What if, instead of walking the uncharted road of spiritual and personal transformation, I had stayed on the well-paved path toward a traditional life?

Maybe then, I thought soberly, I would be in a backyard of my own, with a husband and family. Not unmoored in my childhood bedroom, with the best years already behind me. And how could it *not* be? The tragedy of Gabe's death would be woven into everything that came next.

One humid evening, sitting on the deck eating popsicles with Mom, the subject of marriage and kids came up.

"I thought I had more time," I said tightly, my voice catching. "I was starting to date in that way again— I *was* — but then everything happened with Bubbie, and then Gabe's surgery, and I just—"

"Alee," Mom interrupted gently, "you didn't go the wrong way." She tossed our wooden popsicle sticks into a glass.

"You're feeling this now because you've been completely pulled out of your own life. You did what no woman in this family had done before. You took your time. You felt your feelings. You figured out what you needed."

She smiled and added, "And don't forget, you've already lived an incredible life. The next chapter will come however it comes. But we're able to do this lawsuit, for example, because you became the person who *could*."

I was touched by her words. I needed them.

Before, I could understand why I was on a different timeline than friends or family, especially when Gabe was my ancestral companion on the left-handed path. But after he was gone, it was harder to trust the path at all.

The next week, during an energy healing session on Zoom with Matt, I dropped deeper into those fears. *What if I had lived like there was time, and now I was wrong about that—twice?*

I silently prayed for a change to happen before I jumped out of my own skin. Suddenly, I felt it: a strong, unmistakable breeze in the room. At the same moment, Matt said,

"Don't be afraid of the winds...the winds of change are coming."

As we finished, I looked outside to see rain streaming down, punctuated by sharp cracks of lightning. Hours after I'd gone to bed, a crash jolted me awake. It was the sound of shattering glass.

Mom and I stumbled into the hallway at the same time. Looking down the stairs, we saw that a massive tree had fallen through our skylight, shards of glass scattered across the floor like ice. The humid night air poured through the gaping hole, misting the wood floors, while big green leaves and slender branches floated down like confetti from a broken world.

The winds of change, indeed.

Soon we were in Mom's car, navigating past more fallen trees, the contents of our refrigerator piled in the backseat. The storm had knocked out power across Long Island, but in a true blessing, Celeste had a generator at her house ten minutes away.

I spent the next four days in her guest room with its own bathroom, and it felt like peace.

No childhood bedroom.
No sad photos.
No nostalgia pressing against me like a second skin.

By the third day, I was nearly giddy. I realized I desperately needed a real break from the house, because being somewhere else felt like oxygen. I closed my eyes and asked myself where still felt safe, friendly, familiar, and filled with good memories.

Only one place came to mind.

I opened my laptop and started looking for a sublet in Chicago.

Maybe, just maybe, something there could feel open in a world that was closed.

OCTOBER 2020 CHICAGO, IL

THE CHICAGO STINT

I threw down my suitcases, ran into the first bathroom by the front door, and retched.

It's like that dinner at Aunt Rosemary's, I thought, remembering the intense BBQ meal right after moving everything out of Gabe's.

It felt like all the frustration I'd been holding during those months in New York had slowly gone rancid in my system. Now that I was out of the family house, its presence in my body was undeniable. The tension had started churning in my stomach on the plane ride to Chicago, as I sat with my hands in my lap, mask on, trying not to touch anything.

It was the fall of 2020, deep in the weeds of the Covid pandemic. While most people were canceling their flights, I booked one. I needed to go somewhere — anywhere — that could remind me of a time when I felt like myself, even if it meant simply feeling more like myself alone in a different living room.

Chicago had been the last place I visited in the week before Covid hit the States. Now it was the first place I was going back. I didn't know if it made sense, but I hoped this city might spark happy memories, instead of the agonizing ones that seemed to come the minute I stepped into Mom's house. I still didn't know if I'd ever return to California, the dream I had left Chicago for. My heart had shattered into a million pieces there, and now even the best memories felt bitterly distorted.

I'd taken a two-month sublet in a small building on a spacious, leafy street on the city's West Side. Local friends had checked the place out for me and assured me it was solid. The apartment was the first floor of a family home. They had bought the three-flat back in the '80s, and now it sat in one of Chicago's chicest neighborhoods: Ukrainian Village. It was a place with as many hipster bars stocked with PBR and Malört as there were Eastern European groceries lined with jars of pickled herring and frozen pierogis.

The house sat on a classic block, lined with beautiful old houses, original stained glass windows, wooden porches, and big cement steps that were as solid as they were chipped. It was also my favorite season in Chicago: early autumn, when green leaves burst into shades of gold and coral, and stoops were newly adorned with pumpkins and decorative cobwebs.

Eight weeks to walk the neighborhoods where I had fallen in love three times and experienced some of the biggest spiritual awakenings of my life. This was a city whose rhythm had once lived in my body; where I'd gone dancing all night at street festivals, sat in shamanic dream circles with the old wizard who lived by the lake, hosted raucous potlucks, and cruised through neighborhoods on hazy summer nights, moving from party to party on my bicycle.

It was where I'd eaten steak jibaritos with chimichurri and strong coffee at Cafe Central, and watched ducks glide across the pond as I sat under my favorite tree in Humboldt Park. And it was the only place I could think of that felt like a welcome return.

Still, I prepared for it to feel different than I remembered. It was a pandemic, and most places would be closed, with many interactions happening from feet away with a mask on. And beyond that, four years had passed since I had actually lived in Chicago. In that time, a new era had begun.

The best part of this city had always been the people; innately kind and fun and community oriented. For over a decade, many of my friends were tucked into a cluster of condos and houses in the same few nearby neighborhoods, with a scattering of pals in other parts of the city. But that was a different time.

The great migration of our early thirties had changed that entirely: marriages, babies, and first homes in the nearby suburbs. Other friends—especially my fellow seekers—had drifted to different cities, to try something new. Those who stayed still loved life in Chicago, but the rhythm was different now.

Although the connections remained strong, the once-regular weekend extravaganzas had become special occasions on the calendar—pandemic or not. I couldn't expect anyone's reality to remain exactly as it had been; of course their lives had been changing, too.

I went to flush the toilet and realized I had to press a round electric button embedded in the center of a vinyl record—Chicago, the band, not the city. As I looked around the tiny wicker bathroom, no bigger than a coat closet, I took in the owner's clear devotion to live music. There was a small vinyl collection and framed photographs of rock legends mid-performance—Pearl Jam, Janis Joplin, Bruce Springsteen, Black Sabbath—lined up to the right. To the left, a watercolor of an elderly men's church choir looked down at the toilet with bemused expressions. Although they were only paper, the whole scene created a sense of non-privacy.

I stood up and noticed the final art piece: a painted 3D sculpture of a solar goddess, her face as large as a dinner plate. Part woman, part sun. Triangular, fiery-orange rays splayed evenly in all directions. Her face was round and pale yellow, with bright red tendrils of painted hair and large, sad-looking blue eyes. Pink lips curved into something close to a smirk.

I let out a laugh. She looked eerily like me, if I were bathroom art. Between the address on the heavy wooden door—22, our special number—and the familiar-looking face, I felt a flicker of hope. Maybe I was in the right place. Or at least, maybe this had been the right decision for now.

My apartment was where the adult son of the family kept his collection of art and sculptures from his travels around the world. It was one of the most interesting places I had ever stayed. These creations would soon become my most regular companions for the next two months, more than any other person. Because my loneliness could not be escaped; it traveled with me, especially in a pandemic.

Next to the living room window stood a figure just a few inches shorter than me. It was a Chinese man in ancient warrior robes, sculpted hair parted in the center. One arm was extended as if to shake hands, the other rested at his side, thumb missing. His face was open and kind, with a flat nose, rounded lips, and arched eyebrows. Only after taking in these details did I realize what he was: a replica of a terracotta warrior, the kind made two thousand years ago to accompany emperors into the afterlife.

When I stepped through the bedroom into the main bathroom, I actually cheered. There was a large jacuzzi tub, right beside the classic wavy glass window blocks you see all over Chicago. The tub was wedged a little awkwardly next to the washer and dryer, but now I understood exactly why my friends had vouched for this place for me. That night, I filled the tub and sank into the hot water. I opened the Akashic Records and heard:

Enjoy being in Chicago. You needed the space. But don't try to make this into something it's not.
You're not moving back here.

Then where? I asked. *If not here, then where?*
Florida.

I sat up with a splash. "Bullshit!"

How could God-forsaken *Florida* be where I went next? Beyond the complicated family trips of childhood, it was where Gabe died. It was where I spent the most painful weeks of my life. And yet, underneath the instinctive protests, I could feel the truth. Something about the message clicked in as right, although I simply couldn't imagine why.

The next week, issues started to surface, revealing how unprepared I was psychologically for moving into an old, quirky, unfamiliar space. The dryer blinked and sputtered like it might catch fire. The place hadn't been properly cleaned; crumbs and grime lingered, with no real cleaning supplies in sight. Could there be lingering COVID? Dangerous bacteria? The pillows were aged and stained. And what about the water filter—was it safe?

I replaced the bedding and had a maintenance guy check the dryer. Then I masked up and went to Target for a mop, water filters, cleaning sprays, and towels. When I finally got home, I dropped the bags on the kitchen floor and stared at what my anxiety had deemed necessary for an eight-week stay. I slid down beside them, exasperated with myself

In a Zoom therapy session, I traced the root of the panic and finally named what was happening.

The last time I'd moved into a place, rather than out, was when I helped Gabe set up his apartment in Miami. I recalled the same rising fear, that I had assumed was about me. Standing in Whole Foods, staring at the blue and black candles, wondering if there was something I could do to stop what I was feeling.

My own apartment had been overtaken by mold that I was still recovering from. And now here it was again, that same dread. Could moving in somewhere new kill me? Would *this* apartment be the one?

Gabe had died nine weeks after moving into his.

On the screen, Karin looked over her glasses at me and said,

"Alee, you're most likely safe. But this move is triggering your nervous system. You're remembering what happened before. Be gentle with yourself—especially with what we're *all* living through right now."

A couple of weeks after my arrival, it was an unseasonably warm night, just warm enough to meet my friends at a bar patio for dinner and drinks, which was the only way people were gathering, anyway. I had a salad and two Old-Fashioneds, keeping pace with everyone as we chatted and laughed.

For a moment, it was as if no time had passed: I had never left Chicago, nobody had died, the world wasn't in a viral panic, nothing had changed.

But then it got late. We parted ways, and I walked back across Chicago Avenue. Warm air swept up dry leaves and sand, and the wind pushed the grit against my face. I closed my eyes and kept walking. The light dinner and heavy drinks no longer sat well, and my buzz gave way to anxiety.

My friend Kristina called from L.A. just as I walked in the door. The sound of her voice made my social mask slide off completely. The truth that everything had changed came roaring back into my body. I was *not* okay—not in the way I'd just tried to be. The fun of the night was already a distant memory, replaced by a deep sadness.

My head throbbed, and regret hit me for using alcohol to pretend I was some old version of myself. The cost of that choice revealed itself almost immediately. I hadn't been celebrating; I had been trying to shift my state, to seem happier and lighter in front of my friends. Even though I knew they loved me, I felt self-conscious—about how different their lives were from mine, and about how much I had changed since I last lived here. *And not in a good way*, I thought.

Somehow, it all still felt like a failure of my own making. My heavier body and somber personality felt so vulnerable, like something I needed to apologize for. It made me want to hide behind strong cocktails and old jokes. Now, back in the privacy of my own space, I could feel the truth of that.

Kristina understood more than most. There was no need to pretend or apologize for crying. She had tragically lost her sister in a car accident some years prior.

"I am so afraid to do this in front of anyone," I said between big gulps of air. "I can't let my friends here see this pain. I don't know how I will ever relate to anyone ever again."

She told me about her week, and how the night before she'd gone to a party full of strangers. It happened to be the anniversary of her sister's death. She'd found one person to connect with, and during the conversation, learned that this woman had also lost her sister. Kristina's voice grew quiet and steady.

"It will be okay. I get it. Other people will get it. You will always be close to someone who can get it, wherever you go. There are a million places that can feel like home."

Her words slowed the spinning in my head. I lay on my bed, watching the chandelier cast shifting shadows on the wall. I would probably never be in this room again after the sublet ended, but it would still be an important—if temporary—home; a place to hold me and all these feelings for a stretch of time.

For now, home would be the places where I could let down the performance and simply be where I was at. Lying there, I knew it would be a long time before life felt steady or familiar again. I was too sad for the next chapter I thought I should already be living, and this sadness wasn't something a place or a person could fix. This was the process of recovery.

One social event in Chicago that evaded any pandemic worries was the virtual book club. I had arrived just in time for the Halloween selection: *Mexican Gothic*, a novel about a young woman named Noemí who visits her cousin to meet her strange new fiancé, only to find herself mysteriously unable to leave. She becomes, quite literally, compelled to stay—physically and mentally .

The twist at the end revealed that it wasn't just the creepy family holding Noemí hostage, it was the house itself. A dark, evil ancestral fungus lived in its very walls, entangling and influencing all who entered. As I read, I felt unsettled by the heroine's decline: her inability to resist, to shift anything, or even to try to escape. It reminded me of my time living in Venice, when mold had begun growing in the walls. I could still recall the heaviness, how doing anything felt exhausting, even impossible.

I was curled up on the couch in early November, finishing the final chapter, when my phone rang. It was the office of my new doctor. I had finally found a clinician who didn't skip over the part where I said my symptoms began after living in a house with mold, and he had actually made the time to call me.

In our first appointment, Dr. Zielinkski had studied my blood-work and pointed to what no one else had acknowledged: rapid weight gain, depression, swollen thyroid, allergic reactions, flu-like symptoms were hallmarks of mold exposure.

He explained how the body sometimes tries to protect itself from environmental toxins by storing them in fat, and how that process can wreak havoc on both mood and immunity. He noted that lab markers reflected not just stress but an inflammatory illness. Finally, someone was willing to run the mold labs.

I gripped the cover of *Mexican Gothic* and braced myself for whatever he might say next.

"I'm emailing you the report," Dr. Zielinkski said, "but I wanted to tell you myself. The labs show severe mold exposure. Once mycotoxins enter your system, just leaving the environment isn't enough—they stay with you."

I looked down at the book, struck by the eerie timing, and also not surprised. This was how my life had been speaking to me for years: through undeniable synchronicities, obvious threads I couldn't miss, and sometimes ones that were even darkly funny.

A hot wave of anger rose through me. This poison had been living in my tissues, compounding the stress and inflammation during the most traumatic period of my life. No wonder I had felt so unsafe in both my body and my environment. No wonder I had been so exhausted. It was infuriating that after dozens of appointments, no one had listened to me about the mold for nearly two years, allowing the damage to deepen.

At the same time, I felt compassion for the absurdity of being caught in the middle of a malpractice lawsuit, where Gabe's symptoms had also been underplayed with devastating consequences. And yet here I was, still trying to trust doctors. Still begging them to believe what I already knew in my bones.

There was shame and grief about how much the mold might have been influencing me—how it could have shaped my thoughts, my energy, my body—while I insisted I was okay. My family's fear for my wellbeing was not overblown.

I wondered how it had affected my work. Had the brain fog impacted the quality of my sessions? Made me disorganized with admin or scheduling? I wanted to call everyone who had known me during that year in the apartment and explain. Maybe even apologize.

I couldn't ignore the symbolic parallel: mold as a form of stagnancy. A force that grows in silence, in repression, in spaces held past their expiration date. I knew the deeper purpose of the lawsuit was to help clear out a larger, moldy inheritance—our family's long-standing trauma around betrayal and harm in the medical system. Other relatives had never gotten the accountability or support they needed to heal. But spiritually, we were carrying them forward now.

As I opened the email and read the medical report, I realized something else: I would have to forgive myself.

Forgive myself for not protecting my own well-being.

For not sensing the danger soon enough.

For not having the strength to fight our landlord when the problem was discovered.

For not leaving with urgency until Gabe's death finally pulled me out.

Healing was going to be expensive. But there was also deep relief at having an answer, and a path forward. However long it would take. However much it would cost.

There was a parallel here too. During the same period the mold was wreaking havoc on my body, I had also lost Bubbie and Gabe. Even though the acute crisis had passed, the reverberations were still alive in my tissues, my blood, and my emotional body.

And it would take a long and devoted process for that to change.

DECEMBER, 2020: CHICAGO, IL

THE TRUTH

I sat in the living room, my bare toes tapping on the icy hardwood floor. The air was chilly in that specific way a drafty old house is once winter sets in. I liked the feeling; it kept me alert. As I adjusted myself for the video meeting, I noticed the seven-foot framed rubbing of Joan of Arc behind me, visible on camera like a summoned protector. I liked that, too.

I was leaving the sublet in two days and tried to tuck away the little things I especially appreciated. There had been a few great hangs since that first patio night, like when my friends John and Amanda shared their Mexican traditions for Día de los Muertos with us. Together we'd created a group altar, and a night honoring our dead was something I could step right into, no masking required.

But I had stopped searching for an apartment in Chicago and finally accepted the truth: this had been a respite, not a fresh start. The fresh start wasn't here yet. What lay ahead was a mold detox and a lawsuit entering the stage that would require my full strength and focus.

Mom and I were on a Zoom call with the lawyer we had eventually chosen, a powerhouse named Rhea, with a severe bob and an equally severe presence. It had already been a long road for the three of us.

We'd hired Rhea's firm for Gabe's wrongful death case after an emotional meeting with her associate, Gaetano. He was tender and teary-eyed as he listened to the story, and even told us that his own son was named Gabriel. He also warned us: Rhea wouldn't be as soft as he was. She was harsh, maybe even difficult. 'But,' he said, 'she's who you want in court. Rhea gets the job done.'

Her reputation preceded her, even among our family friends working in New York City law. She was notorious for her steely presence in the courtroom, for shaking even the most unflinching witnesses on the stand. And she wanted our case. After the tedious lead-up of emails, paperwork, and long calls, we believed it wouldn't be long before we were in court and Rhea could do what she did best—the takedown.

But it hadn't gone quite that way.

Covid had slowed everything, sometimes to a total standstill, and a lawsuit was no exception. The endless phase of gathering, printing, and organizing dense documents dragged on. Phone calls. More waiting. Months passed beyond what we expected. I'd sent Gabe's death certificate so many times and to so many email addresses, it had earned its own folder on my desktop.

This was Rhea's least favorite part of the job, and it showed. She was like a tiger in a cage; tense, restless, eager for movement. Her temperament could be sharp and contrary at times, a side of her we'd known since we signed the contract.

At first, I tried to meet her with patience, pleasantly acquiescing to her clipped commands. Over time, I started to snap back, which actually worked better with her. I was finding my own edge, the one I had discovered with Enid last summer

Finally, we were headed toward the real thing. The case would be heard, all relevant parties would be questioned, and eventually, a judgment would be made.

Mom's deposition had been scheduled for the following week. It was time to prepare her for the line of questioning the doctors' lawyers would bring.

"As you know, in New York State, a mother of an adult son would not usually be the one bringing a case forward," Rhea began the meeting.

We knew. The money was never the point—accountability was. But money was how the game worked. And lawyers don't take cases for free; they're paid from the settlement. It turned out every state had different laws around malpractice and wrongful death, like a patchwork of board games, each with its own brutal rules. In New York, it came down to two things: who had been financially dependent on the deceased, and the circumstances of his death.

The very first lawyer we consulted—the tall, suntanned one—had put it plainly:

"What was he worth, and how much did he suffer? That's all that will matter in court. And like I said, it's going to seem very cruel, because the New York State laws are cruel in these kinds of cases. You have to decide if you can handle that."

That had been well over a year ago. At the time, I felt sure I could handle it, that we could handle it. After generations of illness, hospitalizations, and systemic mistakes within the medical system, we were rolling all those experiences into this one case. For Gabe. To reorient the energetic story of a lineage that knew this tale too well.

And yet, as I've learned many times, anything done after a loved one's passing is really for those of us still here, struggling to make meaning, trying to become the people we must now be.

I knew that was true for me. I believed it was true for anyone who's had to keep living after a reality-shattering loss.

This lawsuit was for Gabe. He would have wanted accountability after a life dedicated to improving the healthcare system. But it was also for us, for whatever inner compass was pulling us toward this fight.

It hadn't come without a cost.

I had known I would need to hold both sides: where my brother had been wronged, where the most egregious of outcomes had occurred. And then the part where I trusted the design of life and the deeper knowing that my brother's soul journey was far greater than a doctor's failure. Both.

What I *hadn't* anticipated was having to hold the pose of the victim for so long. To simmer for nearly two years in bitterness, and the hollow disappointment of a world that too often refuses to protect the ones we love.

Rhea fixed her gaze on us through the screen, her thin eyebrows arched.

"You being the ones to bring this type of case forward in New York State is highly unusual," she said. "And so we have to help this court understand why you're here."

I tried to imagine what the lawyers and judge might be picturing that made it seem so unusual, beyond the fact that New York settlements were notoriously lower when the deceased had no spouse or children.

Maybe they pictured a preppy-looking family who hadn't really connected in decades, if ever. The kind who smiled politely for photos, showed up dutifully for holidays, and called each other once a month to catch up on the neighbors. I imagined siblings with a few sweet childhood photos, vague memories of backseat fights, and little else. People who had found their deepest friendships and closest allies out in the world, not in the house they grew up in.

That, obviously, was not us. We had been a tightly woven team for as long as I could remember. All the journeys, losses, and wins — we'd taken them on together. Hysterical laughter in the car and around the dinner table. Inside jokes and phone calls that felt like a deep exhale. Legendary family stories. Surrounding Dad and letting him go.

Gabe and Mom were more than mother and son; they were

dear friends. They met for lunch in the middle of the day and checked in on each other by phone. Mom always said she knew her purpose in life the moment he was born.

For better or worse, there was no one who had more of us than each other. Even when I hated that truth. Even when I compared myself to those seemingly distant families, smiling politely at holidays, building lives away from the people who raised them—it was always there.

And now, somehow, it was surreal to be disqualified, or at least diminished, because we were only his mother and sister.

Rhea continued, her voice even but firm.

"We have to tell the story," she said. "The story of who this family was. How they supported each other. And what the two of you have been through. And that's going to be told—mostly—through how you're questioned."

She looked directly at Mom when she said it.

"Today we'll go through the questions together to practice," Rhea said, "and Alee will be here to give feedback and help answer anything you might forget."

An hour into the questioning, the story began to unfold. What had my parents done for work? Where had they lived? When did they have their children?

Mom's answers started out cheerful, then shifted to melancholy as she recalled the life she and Dad had built, the young family that had felt like a dream come true.

Rhea moved her forward in time to what happened when Gabe and I were teenagers: his initial diagnosis of Hodgkin's Disease, the chemo and radiation, followed by his triumphant transition to college. Then, the shocking follow-up appointment after his first year home:learning the cancer was back, the harsher treatments, the coma he almost didn't wake up from.

The energy in the room tightened. Would one of us finally surrender to the knot in our throats? The tears waiting behind it? It was always sadder to talk about it now, when we knew the ending: neither my gentle and loving father nor my kind and brilliant brother had ultimately survived.

On the heels of Gabe's remission, we had learned that Dad had stage four throat cancer. Rhea asked how it was discovered. Mom kept it steady, just a hint of a waver:

"Well, after those years of working full-time and sleeping at the hospital with Gabe, he figured he was just tired. Actually, it was his band members who insisted he go to the doctor. His singing voice suddenly had this strange gravel to it they'd never heard before. And I remember he… he was snoring more."

Her voice started strong, but as the questioning continued, it got smaller. Then shakier.

Eventually, the answers shifted to: "I don't remember."

And then, the tears came.

It was painful to watch my mother—so much more private than me—give up a life's worth of vulnerable information in such a dry, clinical format. As much as I had processed these events chronologically, to my knowledge, Mom had never described them this way. One moment after another. Without interruption, and without softening.

She didn't trail off or temper the details with humor. She didn't weave the pain into brighter threads, didn't mention the memorial scholarship in my father Chuck's name, or the beautiful songs he'd written, or the many lives Gabe had touched.

For once, those details weren't centered.

For once, the hardest parts stood alone.

This time as I shared the hardships of my high school and college years, they weren't being condensed into the story of why I'd become a healer. Instead, we sat in the other part of the truth: the sadness, the fear, the exhaustion. The holidays spent in hospitals, and the years lived inside a quiet, continuous crisis.

In Mom's answers, I noticed something else, too—she didn't remember my presence in some of the hardest parts of the story.

There were times when I had been home and involved in their

care that she remembered as if I'd been away at college or "somewhere else." In reality, I was still in high school for most of it, and even after I left for college, I came home often when Dad's condition worsened. I wasn't always there, but I was there a lot.

This was a revelation I hadn't known I needed.

For years, I'd carried the sting of feeling unseen. Why had Mom given me such a hard time about needing space from the family? Why had she been so upset about me trying to live my own life, complete with its own dramas that, to her, must have seemed so small?

But something shifted in that moment.

As I watched her finally tell the whole story, I felt a silent, heavy grudge begin to loosen; one I hadn't even realized had shaped my feelings about family and my relationship with Mom for decades.

I saw now that the trauma of losing control over the wellbeing of her beloved family was so acute, so overwhelming, that her memory might have protected me by placing me somewhere else. There had already been so much loss, so much wreckage. Maybe, on some level, it was too much to remember all of it—including me.

For all the times I had felt unseen, there was also so much *I* hadn't fully recognized:

How much pain Mom had held in while buying birthday presents, decorating the kitchen, going to family functions while worrying constantly about her husband or son back at home.

I remembered how hard she tried to make the holidays feel festive, how she would sometimes spend the night in the hospital and drive home on the highway with the truckers at dawn, just to be there when I got up for school. Had anyone truly understood what she was carrying?

Maybe Bubbie, who lived with us.

Because my mother, like her mother before her, did everything she could to keep the resources flowing, to keep the home warm and full and bright. Even with the illness. Even with the fear. She tried to make it a place we'd want to come back to.

How challenging when it felt like it hadn't worked with me.

But there was so much to hold, we couldn't hold it all.

We couldn't always see each other back then.

After a particularly difficult answer about Dad and Gabe's treatment, Mom stopped talking, looked down, and let the tears fall before gently placing her head in her hands. Rhea paused. The questioning stopped, and the silence was full.

I felt guilty for participating; for interrupting with reminders, for saying how hard it really had been. Without the usual layer of spirituality or humor glossed over the top, our story sounded pretty harsh.

And somehow, the moment was exhilarating, too.

I felt seen. I felt acknowledged in a way I never had before.

What was the real impact of having my brother and father in and out of hospitals from the summer after eighth grade through halfway into college?

How often had I downplayed it at parties or in class?

How many times had I sidestepped telling my friends or college crushes why I flew home so often and so spontaneously?

How scary it really had been on those weekends in Huntington, and how conflicted it had felt to return to Boston on Monday mornings, bleary-eyed and hollow.

As I looked at my mother, I sat again with the immensity of what she had endured. Her own father had died of cancer when she was just ten. Decades later, Dad—the love of her life since high school—was gone in middle age, after their son's long and uncertain journey with illness. Along with her father and husband, she had also lost her brother, her mother, and now her beloved son. Each loss had come before she was ready, if one ever can be

It struck me now: both her father and her son—Gabe, whose middle name was *Victor* in his honor—died at the age of 38. Both tied to failures in medicine.

No wonder the message had become so deeply ingrained:

We can never take a break. We can never stop watching. We can never trust someone else with the people we love. This is my job. I am the one to do this. If not me, then who?

When we wrapped up, Rhea was quieter than usual. There was a kind of reverence between us; an acknowledgment of all the family had endured, and of what Mom, as our matriarch, had been carrying for so long.

I logged off and stepped onto the porch, breathing in the cold air. I watched it exhale from my mouth like smoke as the neighbors took down their Halloween cobwebs and paper black cats.

A new season was beginning.

And with it, the next big push of the case.

JANUARY, 2021: LONG ISLAND, NY

THE DEPOSITION

*W*hat *is* the right outfit for being cross-examined about your late brother?

I looked at my reflection. It had been a long time since I'd asked anyone outside my small, safe circle to really look at me. To truly pay attention. It had also been a while since I'd felt beautiful, or like someone who *could* command attention.

And yet right before everything—the apartment disaster, Bubbie's decline, Gabe's death—I had felt *so good* in my skin. I hadn't known how fleeting that might be.

My relationship with my appearance had shifted over the years, often shaped by the weight struggles of my youth, my slightly crooked nose, or the waves in my hair during the stick-straight era of the late '90s and early 2000s.

But as I grew into a young adult, I'd come to see myself as attractive; vitality fueled by a happy life, nourishing meals and long bike rides through whichever city I called home.

A few years of beach living had left me sun-kissed and rosy. My blue eyes held a brightness of curiosity and joy. My reddish-blond waves had lengthened into spiraled curls from daily ocean swims, their ends bleached platinum by salt and sun. I felt like a mermaid.

Before heading out, I'd pause in the mirror, at ease with my strong body and its curves, and the enjoyment in dressing to highlight them. It had taken some time arrive at that place and to embrace myself fully, without judgment or deprivation.

Then came a new season.

I turned thirty-five, and shortly after, my body seemed to unravel. It responded with changes I had never experienced before. There was a distortion in how I now saw my form—both real and imagined.

I became uncomfortably top-heavy. My muscular legs now looked slender next to my upper body. It felt as if the area around my heart was shouting:

I am in pain! I am broken!
There is no more room in this body for all this grief.
I must expand to hold it all.
I need to rage and hide at the same time.
I need to protect my heart.

My face and throat were swollen and pale. My once-bright eyes looked tired and worn. It felt as if I had aged thirty years in fifteen months. There was a downward slope to my face, as if I could cry at any moment. My hair had lost its salt and sun; the red remained, but it was streaked with a dull silvery blonde.

The mermaid magic had washed away.

I tried to summon compassion for what I saw. My body was expressing what I felt and sensed—it was what had made me so powerfully attuned in my healing work. And this physical self had so recently carried the deepest sorrow, anger, and shock it had ever known.

I also knew that with mold illness, many people gain weight as a natural mechanism to keep toxins away from the bloodstream and vital organs. The weight was a sign that my system was protecting me with everything it had while also expressing the truth: Life was heavy.

I wanted to feel gratitude for its brilliance, but it was hard.

The voices inside were loud:

You didn't appreciate your beauty when you had it.
You wasted it on the wrong men, at the the wrong time.
Now you'll be alone, too weathered and sad to be desired again.

I felt exposed in my brokenness. That anyone who looked at me could tell. And I hated that I felt that way—because if this were a client, a friend, or a family member, I would deeply admire them for surviving what I had, for what this body had.

But the the younger version of me, the one who had tried to keep up, to cry silently, to be inspirational instead of tragic—she was terrified. Terrified that the way I looked now meant nothing had been true.

If this could happen to Gabe; if this could be where I landed after decades of researching and applying every "right" way to heal, grow, and do the hard things...

What had it all been for?!

For the first time, nothing I tried could produce the external results I thought I needed to feel better. There was no magic bullet to speed through the parts I hated. Nothing could bring Gabe back or undo what had happened. I had finally met the metaphorical dragon who had slayed me. And if my worth was only found in saving the day, what good was I now?

The toll of the last couple years had created a physical expression that was dense and unyielding. It could not be pushed into changing by eating or *not* eating, by movement, meditation, mindset, or any supplement on the shelf.

At my last tearful appointment, the doctor had looked at me gently and said,

"Please try to understand. This is your body in a state of trauma, and it doesn't feel safe yet. It won't release the toxins *or* the weight until it feels secure to do so."

A release requires an opening. I wasn't ready to open.

I wondered if the legal staff and lawyers would see what I saw. Would anyone take my opinions on health seriously? Ironically, I was learning and implementing more than ever before.

But to me, it sure didn't look like it.

I put on my soft black jumpsuit with the floral kimono-style jacket that I'd worn to Gabe's funeral, and later to those first meetings with the lawyers. Right now these were the clothes that fit well and had already carried me through some nerve-wracking events.

Next a quick swipe of natural-colored makeup and styling of my hair, which I'd blown out straight. I didn't wear my usual long waves, lest I seem any more like the "nutty spiritual sister" than I already did.

I came downstairs to the kitchen, which looked out to a blustery blue sky and tree branches slick with a shining coat of ice. This deposition had become the only thing I could cling to during the dark winter and my recent return to Huntington from Chicago —a leap that had felt like a flop, after spending a second holiday isolated in grief.

If I could just get to this meeting, maybe it would crack something open. Maybe they would recognize the truth, and I could do something that mattered: speak up on behalf of Gabe.

I looked at the clock. 10:07 a.m. It was Monday. Gabe had died around this time on a Monday morning. I'd read somewhere that this was the most common day and time for heart attacks.

The week before, after another legal meeting, Mom and I had come home and turned on the news. People were storming the Capitol. They yelled and screamed, faces twisted with rage and adrenaline, feet up on desks. The world was growing more unhinged by the day. But nothing really surprised me anymore.

My brother's friends kept texting that they wished they could hear his grounded take on it all, and I wished for that, too.

As my coffee brewed, I reached for a plate. It slipped from my hands and shattered into white shards on the floor. Bubbie used to say a broken plate meant good luck. I hoped it was that, and the release of something not meant for this meeting.

Mom and I drove to the law office together. Because of COVID precautions, my deposition would take place at the Long Island branch of our firm, with the opposing lawyer questioning me through the softened layer of a Zoom screen. Part of me was relieved and part of me worried it might dull the impact of what I had to say.

Mom couldn't observe, so she waited outside. Like a parent on the first day of school, she gave me a big, teary hug and sat as close as she could.

I entered the glass conference room where a large screen hung above the table. Janis, a lawyer from this branch's office, sat beside me instead of Rhea. She was older, with long blonde hair, crinkled eyes, and a kind smile that put me at ease. I was glad it was her. As everyone settled in, I closed my eyes and opened the Akashic Records. My body softened. Light surrounded the room.

You've got this.

Just say what's true—nothing more, nothing less.

You don't owe them more than that.

When the Zoom window opened, I saw myself seated at the head of the table in a red leather chair. I looked... composed. Cool. Like I had it together.

Then the doctor's lawyer appeared. She was a middle-aged woman with short brown hair, wearing a navy blazer. But instead of an office, she seemed to be in a dimly lit room with a sliding wooden cupboard door behind her.

Wait—*was* she actually in a snack cupboard?

I soon realized it was more like a small side room, because midway through her first set of questions, a little boy came sprinting across the screen, giggling. A German shepherd chased behind him, barking playfully.

"Christopher!" she scolded, sighing as she got up and shut the door again.

She turned back to the camera with a sheepish smile.

"Sorry, they're home from school today, and with us not being able to go into the office..."

I wanted to laugh.

All that preparation, all those deep breaths as I imagined some icy, high-powered lawyer trying to rattle me, while a stern judge banged a gavel and yelled, "Order in the court!"

Instead I was across from a frazzled working mom Zooming in from wherever she could find privacy. So far my own lawyer had been more intimidating to me in our meetings.

During breaks, both sides chatted casually. For them, it was just another day. For me, it was something else. I realized I could choose what this moment meant: for me, for Gabe, for our family. Because no one in that room was going to make it more or less intense than it was.

Still, this was my opportunity to speak. Gabe had followed this doctor's exact advice, and he had died following it, in the prime of his life. There was *nothing* casual about that.

"Did your brother ever practice... energy work?" she asked.

Jesus. What is this, the Salem Witch Trials?

"Do you mean his Qigong practice? It's been used as a healing art for centuries. Gabe did practice it—but always alongside his doctors' care, including his cardiologist's."

She looked down at her notes and continued.

"Did your brother speak at an event called *The Functional Forum?*"

She was referring to Gabe and Maskell's monthly gathering for doctors and practitioners. It had been a lively public exchange of ideas, new models, and innovations in healthcare. The recordings were posted on YouTube, so I assumed someone on their side had looked it up.

"Yes," I replied.

"And did your brother give a talk..." She scanned her papers. "...called *Cancer is a Myth?*"

Of course. It had been a *Forum* event on oncology care. As a two-time cancer survivor, Gabe had opened the evening with a personal speech. To anyone wanting to paint him as a guru who believed cancer could be denied away by positive thinking, the title was a goldmine. But the talk wasn't about cancer being fictitious.

"If you listen to the talk, it's not about 'myth' as in untrue," I said, my voice trembling with restrained frustration. "It's about mythology—like the Hero's Journey Joseph Campbell wrote about? Gabe was speaking to the idea that cancer could be experienced as a modern version of that journey. That each patient could be the hero of their own path."

Her eyebrows lifted; not in challenge, but in interest.

I wanted to say, *Yes, it's really good. Maybe you should actually watch it instead of just quoting the title.*

But I held my tongue.

Keep it moving.

They don't need to understand.

Just answer the questions.

The deposition continued. The lawyer looked for openings, searching for any angle where this tragedy could be a result of Gabe's carelessness. Because that was her job.

My mantra to these inquiries became,

"Not to my knowledge, no."

I repeated it over and over in response to questions that made me want to scream. But I felt Gabe and Dad close by and their presence steadied me.

In another life, this would have been our new inside joke. Creating a catchphrase out of something absurd or painful—that was quintessential to our family's humor. We would've been repeating it to each other for the next month:

"Not to my knowledge, *no*," with our brows comically furrowed, as if auditioning for a legal drama on TV.

If they had still been alive.

Finally, she asked her last question—something about his health routine—and I added, "He was especially careful. We all were, after what he and my father had gone through."

The hearing was adjourned. Janis squeezed my hand. "You did great. Exactly how you want to answer."

I drove home with Mom. The whole thing felt anticlimactic, and maybe that was a blessing. How much more intensity did we need?

Two days later, Rhea emailed asking for recent photos of Gabe, preferably with family. She said the doctor had claimed in his deposition that Gabe looked "unhealthy" at his appointment.

So untrue.

I sent a photo from the year before they died: Bubbie, Mom, Gabe, and me, standing in the sunshine, sunglasses on, arms around each other. My brother looked fit, his smile wide.

How could it be that Mom and I were the only ones left?

None of this brought the closure I had hoped for.

No one involved would care like we did.

And Gabe would still be gone.

MARCH, 2021: HUNTINGTON, NY

THE CLOSING ARGUMENT

*T*he rest of the winter felt bleak, particularly as we passed through Gabe's second posthumous birthday. He would have been 40. What would he have done for the milestone occasion?

I baked chocolate cupcakes with homemade frosting and birthday candles. We set one in front of a photo of Gabe, his arms outstretched in the frame. When we lit the candle and began to sing Happy Birthday, the flame flickered against the glass, reflecting right at the center of his heart.

One morning in early March, Rhea called. Her voice was fast and serious.

"I'm on Zoom with the doctor's lawyer and the judge. They want you to join us right now, so please get to a computer."

"Right now?" my mother sputtered. "But we're not ready. We had no idea that—"

"*Hurry*," said Rhea. "This is a *very* important, highly respected judge and she's already on, and—"

Mom and I looked at each other and understood that it was likely everyone wanted us a little off-kilter and unprepared. They were ready to make a deal, and no one wanted to give us too much time to think.

"Okay," I said firmly. "We'll be on shortly, but we need a minute."

I was done being intimidated by our lawyer or anyone else involved in this case. Nothing was scarier than what had already happened. And no one, not even the most respected judge, had the power to change that.

When Mom and I joined the video call, everyone was already on camera: Rhea, the doctor's lawyer and the judge herself.

She was an older woman with spiky short hair, spiral earrings, and what looked like her around-the-house loungewear. She reminded me of the whimsical-crunchy older women I used to love seeing at the Portland airport. But her voice was crisp and no-nonsense.

The judge fixed her eyes on us without a smile.

"I wanted to have you on,"she said, "because we're coming to the point where this wraps up. And because of Covid, I can hold this kind of meeting with you directly.

Something you've likely already discovered is that there is no justice here. But there *can* be accountability. There can be an acknowledgment, at least in some way, of what happened."

It was surreal to hear her say it so plainly, to realize that everyone involved already knew the truth.

"Well... this certainly hasn't been *Law and Order*," I said.

I felt so stupid the moment the words left my mouth that I almost laughed at myself. But it was true.

The collective fantasy of a lawsuit—shaped by years of TV dramas where the good guys prevail and everyone is devoted to truth and justice—was far from reality. In truth, it was more of a mundane process and, ultimately, a business.

They invited us to speak.

Mom went first. Her voice broke as she spoke of her beloved

son, his presence in the world, and the way this loss had changed *everything*.

Then the doctor's lawyer —"Lawyer Mom" from my deposition —began to offer a statement about how her client couldn't *possibly* have known what would happen if—

"Excuse me," I interrupted. My voice came out low and steady. "I just want to remind everyone what actually happened."

The group stilled, and I continued.

"Gabe had surgery. He attended his post-op appointments and followed every single medical recommendation. Even after all the trauma with Western medicine, after everything he and my dad had gone through. He trusted these doctors. He *believed* them."

I looked directly into the screen.

"He believed the cardiologist when he told him to walk on the treadmill. He believed him when he said the feeling was just anxiety. He even believed him when he insisted the stress test wasn't urgent. And he literally died doing the thing your client told him to do. Your client never told Gabe he could be in danger. He never said—"

I paused. On the screen, the lawyers and judge were all wincing, shoulders tightening like they were bracing for impact.

The judge cut in, her voice measured but insistent. "Yeah, we can't get into that. That's considered hearsay."

I blinked. Oops.

"Oh," I said. "Well, that's it, then. That's all I wanted to say. And I appreciate that you let me do it."

I exhaled, sinking back into my chair with a long sigh of relief. It felt cathartic to speak without waiting for permission—to finally name what had happened, instead of being confined to clipped, careful answers to questions designed to keep me from saying too much.

There was a little more conversation, and then the meeting wrapped. Essentially, the lawyers and the judge wanted to close this up. There would be no real winners. Someone wonderful had died in the prime of his life.

And wonderful or not, like anyone else, he had deserved appropriate medical care. He deserved accurate information, and to be listened to when he described his symptoms and concerns.

As for the doctor, this academically and professionally esteemed cardiologist now had a tragic misstep imprinted on his legacy, right at the end of his career. I figured that's what kept him clinging to his easily disproven testimony. I had a shred of understanding, if not compassion.

I still wanted to punch him in the face.

Financially, it seemed there would also be no meaningful "win." The laws of New York State ensured that. That's why this meeting had been called—so that hopefully, Mom and I would at least feel seen and heard, in anticipation of how offended we'd likely be by the settlement offer.

Of course, we could always hear the number, reject it, and wait for a trial. But Rhea looked at us soberly as she laid out the landscape.

"I want you to know," she said, "a trial could take *years* to happen, especially with all these new Covid delays. And the jury could reject the claim entirely, or lower whatever we might get here. New York City jurors are full of doctors, lawyers, people with ties to this *specific* hospital."

Everyone involved wanted to be done.

There was to be no satisfying ending for anyone. Rhea the Tiger had already had her successful day in court—driving the doctor out of the deposition room and the hospital into settlement negotiations. That's why we were in this meeting.

The truth was that I wanted to be done, too

I knew that holding an extended pose of victimhood wasn't healthy. But there had been no other way to stay in the fight for this long. How else do you survive a wrongful death lawsuit for over two years? The whole premise is that something *wrong* happened. Before this, my family had never allowed ourselves to wallow here.

"You can tell when someone finds out about your diagnosis," Gabe had said in his *Cancer Is a Myth* talk,

"They look at you like they're just **so** relieved to not be you.
It's the worst feeling, when someone does that.
So if you can't see someone as the hero of their own story, step off.
Get out of the way, and let them move forward.
Never bring that energy to someone doing battle."

I'd always thought people weren't actually sorry for Gabe—they were in awe of him. Of his courage and his grounded, playful presence. Of his unwavering devotion to helping others have an easier time than he had. Maybe they couldn't imagine responding that way in those circumstances.

And yet, I knew what he meant.

I'd had my own version of that experience when we were younger: trying to persevere, make the best of it, and hide how scared or stressed I really was. But it wasn't only about avoiding the role of victim. My whole family had wanted to enjoy and to create, to make meaning of our experiences—even the hard ones. If I had felt perpetually sorry for everyone, I wouldn't have been able to live the way I wanted to. And I wouldn't have been honoring my dad's and brother's wishes, either.

After Dad died, I did have one big surge of guilt and shame for not appreciating the song he had written for me on his final album. It was a breezy acoustic track called *Proud of You*, and it mentioned various moments from my life. The chorus went like this:

> *Any fool can ride a wave,*
> *end up on the sand*
> *But when things get tough*

do they have enough
to play out their hand?
Now you've left the nest,
passed the test,
you hold the Ace of Spades
And anyway
it doesn't pay
to be afraid
Oh, I'm so proud of you
and the things you do
But it's the true friend you are—that's the most important
thing by far

In the months after Dad died, I would play the song on loop on my Discman when I was sad. I'd feel comforted yet riddled with guilt.

"I didn't appreciate him enough!" I cried to Mom through tears. "He wrote me a song—and it was so beautiful—and I didn't even, like, *thank him*–thank him. And I still got annoyed with him sometimes. I still wanted to go hang out with friends when I was home and—"

"Alee!" Mom had said, her voice rising with conviction. "That was exactly the right way to be.

Dad didn't want you treating him like he was fragile or about to die. He didn't want you to stand on ceremony with him, he was your *father*.

And he wanted you to be just like that, to keep living. That's what made him happiest—to know you were still able to do that, even with everything going on."

These days, I wondered if I *had* actually continued living on the way they assumed.

But back then, her words gave me some relief and the guilt receded. And over time, I came to understand that Dad hadn't written the song so I could praise him. Of course not. He'd written it for later on—when it would be the only way he could still tell me he was proud.

And yet, I didn't always know how to feel proud, or to treat myself with the gentleness my history required; far more gentleness than I believed I could allow while succeeding.

The same conflict showed up in my relationships, especially where healing and business overlapped. I wanted care and accountability, and I also assumed anyone devoted to healing would embody integrity—that they would treat another's fragility with respect and never exploit vulnerability for profit.

But it wasn't always like that. Some carried their own shadows into the work, cloaked in the language of healing.

When disappointments came, Gabe seemed able to shake them off. Me? It felt like I kept a shit list etched into my psyche. And still, whenever something felt off or out of pocket, I assumed it had to be me—something I'd said, done, manifested. My reflex was always to try harder to make it right.

It was too frightening to admit when something hurt. Too frightening to risk rejection, disappointment, or triggering someone else. Terrifying to face the possibility that my choices might not have been the right ones—or worse, that they hadn't mattered at all. Because that would mean I wasn't in control.

Eventually I ran out of tokens, the ones that kept me silent, kept me hiding my anger, kept me convinced I was responsible for everything. Not acknowledging the pain had become unsustainable.

The collapse that finally came was the very thing my body and soul had been preparing for. On some level, I had always known it would come. In that sense, letting myself descend into the truth that my family had been wronged was healing.

And allowing for the possibility that Gabe—who I had once believed knew *everything*—could have been misinformed or mistaken was, in its own way, a release. Easier to bear than believing the only person I could ever rely on for truth was gone forever.

My brother had been **extraordinary**. But he didn't need to be omniscient, superhuman, or godlike. He could simply be what he was: beautifully human.

Through the lawsuit, I began to loosen the grip. To stop trying to control every moment and outcome, and then silently stew in the resentment I refused to name.

In some karmic way, taking legal action felt like retribution; not just for Gabe, but for generations of pain. For the ones who never had the words, the witnesses, the chance to name what had happened.

And yet, outside of the lawsuit, I had never felt so unsure of my place in the world. The structures I had invested my faith and resources into were crumbling. And although the case was winding down, I realized I would still have to hold two poses for a while longer:

The part of me that trusted in the perfection of divine order,
And the part of me that felt I'd been sold a lemon of a life.

That night, after the Zoom meeting with the judge and lawyers, I carried it all into what had become my sanctuary in the house. The first-floor den, once our family TV room, now held framed photos of Gabe and Dad, flanked by their records and spiritual totems.

A tall wooden bookcase stood against the far wall, filled with their literary collections: biographies, music, healing, spirituality. The room was almost completely dark except for a string of small, multi-colored Christmas lights casting a soft pink glow.

Opposite that wall sat a wooden work table with my computer and what I called The Gabe Station: his laptop, his phone, and a cardboard box crammed with the paperwork I'd been dutifully collecting and filing: taxes, contracts, medical records, his death certificate. Everything that officially confirmed he had lived, existed, made choices in the world.

Beneath the table sat my free weights and a rolled-up infrared sauna bag. Behind the chair loomed a Peloton bike, the at-home workout craze of Covid. Sometimes, the perky instructors felt like my only friends.

Most evenings I retreated to this space to sweat, cycle, and sometimes cry in the dark. The sauna steamed up the icy windows while trees whistled outside. Occasionally raccoons rattled the trash cans, testing whether I'd properly weighed the lids down with rocks. Nighttime was when I could fully relax; shielded from the daylight's pressure to engage, produce, be visible.

Tomorrow, both sides would begin negotiating the settlement.

That past week, I'd felt an unexpected pull to rewatch all three Lord of the Rings movies. I'd only seen them once before, a decade earlier, snowed in during a blizzard with my boyfriend at the time, who was an epic fantasy enthusiast.

I could hardly remember the plot, but when a film started to magnetize me like that, I knew it was carrying a message meant for the moment I was in. So, I surrendered to the full trilogy— hours of immersing myself in the Hero's Journey of it all. I was especially touched by the brotherhood among the men, and by the quiet, fatherly protection of Gandalf. But it was one particular conversation between Frodo, the bearer of the burden of the ring, and the old wizard that landed the deepest:

"I wish the ring had never come to me," Frodo said. "I wish none of this had happened."

And Gandalf replied:

"So do all who live to see such times. But that is not for them to decide.

All we have to decide is what to do with the time that is given to us."

Tears welled in my eyes the first time I heard those lines.

I, too, wished none of it had happened.

But it had.

And now I needed to find the strength to understand why I felt so burdened by this role. I turned off the TV, closed my eyes, and sank into the Akashic Records.

It was time to uncover the story beneath the story.

When I opened the Records, I asked for insight into my soul's connection to this lawsuit. Why had it fallen to me to carry this?

Images spun through my mind like a slot machine until they landed on a scene:

A courtroom, generations ago. An elderly woman stood at the plaintiff's table in a simple dress and shawl. She was the last surviving member of her family, there to represent her late husband and son—both part of a line marked by injustice.

These men, like others before them, had worked for equality and healing. And now she stood for them, determined to say no to the curse that haunted their bloodline. Her determination mirrored my own.

The scene froze. Her eyes, bright with light, met mine.

"Do not be afraid," I felt her say. *"We, as women, must stand for them. Not to bring them back, but because their lives mattered. We have the strength to speak, even if it feels lonely. This is their gift to us: who we become through this moment, and whatever prosperity follows. They want this for us—the ones still here."*

The woman's presence was powerful and grounded. She had made that courtroom work for them and with them.

"What will happen with the settlement in my timeline?" I asked silently.

"You will be offered less at first," she said. *"Don't accept it. It isn't the truth."* She revealed the number they would later offer, then offered to help me expand the possibility to a higher number.

I felt the settlement's energy in my field; it was dense and electric. With her guidance—and the presence of the Akasha—we lifted and stretched it, until it felt complete.

I offered my gratitude and asked for anything else I should do.

"Be there for your mother," she said. *"This is a pivotal moment—one that will change her life. **It's okay** to let go tomorrow. This chapter is about healing for both of you. It isn't about making things right for Gabe. He has already moved on. This is for you all now."*

When I emerged from meditation, the chill in the room made me pull my blanket tighter. In the years when everything in my life seemed to burn away, I had wanted to reject it all. But my connection to the Akasha had endured through those flames, guiding me even through the most devastating truths. I trusted this encounter had already shifted something that would be revealed in the morning.

The next day, our lawyer called: they had offered the lower number I'd seen in the Akashic experience.

"But I told them to go back and *think* about themselves before they insult us all with that," Rhea snapped, her voice sharp with flair.

She wasn't wrong—especially since the firm would take a third of whatever we settled for. Later came another call: a slightly higher offer. Rhea urged us to take it.

But I remembered what I'd seen the night before. *This isn't the real number.* So we refused.

"They might say no," Rhea cautioned, though she promised to press them again.

Mom and I sat together in the living room. The day was unseasonably warm and a little stuffy as sunlight streamed through the windows. I could feel it—the beginning of the end of this chapter.

The lawsuit had become my north star, the place where I directed my purpose, my energy, my need to create meaning.

For Mom, it was a channel for her love. A way to account for what had happened at Gabe's final doctor's appointment. A moment where she knew something was wrong but the doctor dismissed her. Despite her fierce medical advocacy and relentless devotion to both Gabe and Dad over the years, she couldn't change their fates.

They were hers to love, but not to save.

Until now, Mom had mostly avoided the money discussions. For her, this was never about gain; it was about accountability. But she had also seen what the process had cost me, and how we'd been treated along the way. Today, she was different.

As we waited for our lawyer's next call, she sat up straight and declared, voice steady over the speakerphone:

"For everyone else, this is just about money; it's their job, their work. And if that's the only way they can show accountability for what happened to Gabe, then I'm ready to ask for it."

She was speaking to Kenny, the family friend and attorney who had been with us at the start. I heard him reply:

"Of course, Gina. Just know they won't exceed the standard payout in these cases. They don't want to set a new precedent."

Mom set her mug down gently. "Well, someone has to set a precedent eventually, right?"

She paused—just as Rhea beeped in again.

"Gotta go, they're calling!"

Rhea didn't waste time sharing the new number before saying,

"That's their *final* offer. They'll go to trial otherwise. And just so you know, it's three times what they originally intended to pay."

My thoughts went back to the night before: this was the figure my soul guide had revealed in the energy process. *This is it. Say yes.*

Mom ended the call, saying we'd discuss and get back to her. She turned to me, uncertain. "I'm not sure if we should take it."

My mother had reclaimed her power through this process, shedding the shame and secrecy that had silenced others in our family for generations. To ask for accountability, to hire a lawyer, to request compensation—this had been new for her. And trans-formative.

The truth was, after all we'd been through, the settlement mattered and would be a support. It wasn't just symbolic. And for Mom, this would be the last step she could take in the world to make sense of that awful day, of not being able to protect her son.

"Mom," I said softly. "Let's take it. If it's more than they've ever given before, then we *did* set a precedent. And if we said no, we'd just be delaying this for another year."

They had already warned us the backlog could drag things out for months or years, even after acceptance. Mom agreed. She called a close friend to share the decision, and I heard her say quietly, almost like a prayer:

"It's time for Alee to stop thinking about this all the time."

I wondered what I would think about instead.

We called our lawyer and confirmed. She had been firm during negotiations, but now her tone softened. As she explained the next steps, I watched the sun sink through the blinds, the weight of finality settling in. Before we hung up, she said:

"I want you to know that it was your work here that made a difference. Everything you both did, and the powerful story of your family, created this unusual outcome." She cleared her throat. "And listen, I... know I can be difficult. But this is how I have to be. I sit with people all day, every day, in the worst times of their lives. If I wasn't like this, I think I would die."

There was a deep exhale from both of us. For the first time, we could sense Rhea outside of her role.

I felt a warmth in my heart and a slow unwinding in my mind as I extended that realization outward to everyone involved in the case. Mom and I would bear the scars, but they were ours to bear. These were our people. Our blood. We would never again partici-pate legally in the sorrow and gravity of the worst possible mistake. But Rhea and the lawyers were already moving on—new cases, new families, new heartbreak.

We hung up.

"So that's it," Mom said lightly.

We stood, stretched, and decided to walk around the block; the walk we had taken so many times with Gabe, Bubbie, and Dad that our neighbors called it *The Hoffman Family Constitutional.*

The air felt different. There was no more wondering, no more waiting to know the ending of the story.

For this, I swelled with pride. Gabe and I had always planned to help Mom with her retirement. And now, even after the third that would go to the lawyers, there would be a nest egg. The first one Mom had been given after a lifetime of loss.

From that first meeting, when we were told we probably couldn't do this, as *only* his mom and sister, to now.

It was finished.

We had carried it all the way through.

JULY, 2021: SOMEWHERE IN PENNSYLVANIA

THE NEW WAY

"*A*ttention! If you remove your mask, even while sleeping, you *will* be dropped off at the next stop!"

I sighed. It was stuffy and uncomfortable, but also the only way to be in an enclosed capsule with hundreds of other people in the year 2021. My thoughts drifted back to my last journey on this same train.

No masks, no *concept* of Covid, let alone talk of it.

We had walked freely through the crisply air-conditioned cars, and Mom had sipped a gin and tonic at the curved retro bar car with jolly red leather booths.

Lovely in theory, but at the time I had enjoyed none of it. I'd been too exhausted from the previous days of moving and driving in the heat. Too horrified by the fact that we were bringing everything *back* just three months after Gabe and James had taken the same train to bring it *there*.

On that last train trip, I had wanted to disappear, but settled for sitting somberly in my seat and dissociating through David Sedaris audiobooks. I remembered the white-clothed table in the dining car with the two strangers paired with us; the overly cheerful

Disney woman who wanted everyone to go around and say why we were on the train. Now, I could tell her.

In fact, I'd be *happy* to tell her.

All those pleasantries had felt like torture when we were transporting Gabe's belongings and his urn of ashes from Florida back to New York. And now, ironically, none of those amenities were even available. The train itself was barely operational. No walking between train cars, no pretend-fancy dinner service, no snack stands near the bar. In fact, no food or drinks at all, besides water. Mom and I hadn't known that when we boarded the 17-hour ride; this time we'd brought nothing, assuming we would get food onboard.

Mom rifled through her purse and emerged with an ancient mini bag of trail mix and an orange.

"Well, this time, not only would I have been okay with the mystery date dinner," I said, rolling my eyes, "but we actually *need* your crazy deli food."

The infamous turkey sandwich from 3Gs Deli in Delray Beach —the pit stop that had just enough time for us to miss boarding our original train. This time, we just looked at each other and laughed. We could handle struggles as a duo now. We didn't feel victimized by experiencing them together, nor was our first instinct to project our frustrations onto each other.

Somewhere in this long container of time—the long road trips, managing the unhinged tenant, the sorrowful holidays where no one seemed to understand, the abrasive lawyer meetings, the planning and execution of multiple funerals and memorials, the late nights of tears and bad movies and dark humor—something had shifted.

We had learned how to lean on each other instead of lashing out. We had become the new iteration of our family team.

It was the kind of connected mother–daughter relationship Mom had always wanted, and the one I had spent years in personal growth spaces trying to form.

"It just took everyone dying, is all," I sometimes joked, cryptically.

Of course, there were still arguments and frustrations. These had been hard years—for *everyone*, not just us. Sometimes I shut down and disconnected, got in my head and worried about becoming a middle-aged woman whose only companion in life was her mother.

Sometimes Mom still projected her frustrations onto me, or wanted me to stay in a safe, small life that she and her anxiety could sign off on—one where **nothing else** could happen to her family. Understandable, given what she'd lived through. But I needed to feel like I could live *my* life.

And sometimes she wanted the kind of presence that would take a whole brood to provide, and right now it was just down to me.

Maybe it was a Jewish thing, but the matriarchs on my mother's side always seemed to hit a certain stride in their later years— when they were finally catered to and cared for after decades of being the rock for everyone else. By the whole family, of course, but especially by their daughters.

From my great-great-grandmother on, the Bubbies of our lineage moved into their daughters' homes. Their wellbeing and logistics were managed while they offered doting time with grandchildren and held court as revered tradition-keepers during the holidays. My great-grandmother had it with her own mother. Then the onus passed to Bubbie. And then, inevitably, to Mom.

But I couldn't offer that traditional Jewish daughter's path. I didn't have other immediate family members to help share the labor. I didn't have the husband and children for her to fuss over— though I hoped to one day. And I didn't want to stay enclosed in that dynamic either, because that part of the old way wasn't true for us.

Mom wasn't going to *be* Bubbie; the docile grandmother sipping coffee in her mother-in-law apartment, waiting to be asked her opinion. She and I had inherited the strength of our feminine line. We had endured many of the same deep losses and disappointments, and something in us had been built to survive it.

But Mom carried a different kind of fire. She had the warmth and magnetism to attract lifelong friends like Bubbie, but she could also be volatile under stress. When I was younger, I resented this. Why did she have to flare while Bubbie was ever-smiling and pleasant? Bubbie's friendly greeting was so iconic that imitating it became a family pastime:

"*Children!*" she'd exclaim to anyone younger than 95. "How *are* you, my darlings?"

After supporting Bubbie through her dying process, I came to understand more. As incredible as she was, she had also repressed much of her reasonable anger. And as a result, her daughter had carried it for her—and expressed it.

My mother.

There hadn't been space for rage, grief, or depression to be openly acknowledged then—not without risking disconnection from surviving family and friends. Back then, people believed it was better not to discuss loss with children. As if they wouldn't feel it, so long as it wasn't spoken aloud.

Mom told me that for years, she believed her hardworking, happy father must have been a spy on a secret mission. How else could he have just *disappeared* when he loved them all so much? She told me Bubbie had been advised not to let her three children —ages six, ten, and thirteen—attend their father's funeral. Other kids at school even teased them for not having a dad anymore.

Still, Bubbie's house became the gathering place: birthdays, holidays, everyday joys. Years later, that house would become my parents' home. Then Gabe's places. Then my own string of city apartments scattered across the country.

No matter where we lived, the mission stayed the same: to keep going and to keep joy alive.

The origin story of *Dark Times Catering.*

Because our crew, even with all its loss, had always known how to bring the warmth. To fill a room with laughter, storytelling, music, and something to nosh on. It was our historical talent, so innate, as we truly loved people. And yet also it was also our way for safety. Keep everyone happy. Keep them close.

Though many beautiful memories came from that, there was also a cost. Keeping everything down to keep moving on had left older generations unfamiliar with how to face harsher emotions together, leaving undigested pain in its wake.

Gabe and I made it our life's work to break that pattern, though it still was a work in progress. We wanted to dig into the full spectrum of feelings, to play all the notes. To trace the family imprints that shape a life, and to tie up the karmic loose ends.

I remembered standing with Gabe at Bubbie's grave that January, thinking of her and our grandfather, we only knew through spirit and stories, Victor. She had ended up passing away on the same day as him, *60 years later.* We were so sure we had done our part. So sure we had untethered our family from the generational curses, so sure we could expand into a whole new way of being. We hadn't known that Gabriel Victor himself had just three months left.

After I moved back to Huntington, I found our grandfather's death certificate in the basement. Not only had he and Gabe died at the same age of thirty-eight, but it had also been the same time: 10:15. He was p.m. Gabe was a.m.

It was devastating to think that even after everything we tried to be conscious of, my brother's loss was one more way it would still be like the past. One more death that came too soon, another crack in the system that widened into a chasm. It echoed everything we had grown up hearing about our Zeidi Victor. And later, when people spoke about Dad:

"If only he were still here, everything would be different. It all could have worked out."

But I was still here.

What could *I* do differently?

Those were the questions that rose after Gabe died. And while I might collapse in a thousand other ways, I couldn't run from this. I wouldn't turn my back on the devotion we had both shared to finding the answers. He had worked too hard. We both had.

If this was his fate—if Gabe's spirit had taken on the sacrifice of the other men in our family—then how could I, through the feminine lineage, commit to a different destiny for all of us?

The lawsuit had been one doorway.

For every woman in our family who should have had access to legal counsel and reparations. For every man who should have received better medical care and been able to leave more behind for the family he loved and worked so hard for.

And for me—for us—that pursuit of accountability became a threshold into who we could become in the process.

Ultimately, I knew that to truly honor what I had learned from Gabe, I had to learn to be with Mom differently. To recognize that he and Dad were gone, and they had left me to finish some things on their behalf.

I could either deny that and feel victimized, or take it on as the embodiment of what I claimed my soul work to be in this world.

What would they have done?

I learned how to extend myself to support my mother's wellbeing. To handle more logistics, take on some physical labor, and to joke with her in a way that felt loving—not sharp or defensive. There was a new maturity and grounding in me: less overwhelm, a wider capacity.

For a while, I had thought I was being "the man of the house" by staying with Mom. But I see now—I wasn't performing masculinity. **I was stepping into my next stage of womanhood.**

I chose my mother; both as a parent and as my friend. That had been Gabe's way with her. And while I couldn't offer a mother-in-law suite or grandchildren to shop for, I could offer that.

In turn, Mom gave me what I hadn't realized I'd been waiting for all along:

To be heard and seen.
To feel that my mother's view of me could be a safe space.
To be understood and validated.
To be recognized for how much I had carried for this family.
To be celebrated for the way I had worked to make meaning of our story, while also building one of my own.

If I hadn't fought for my own path, I wouldn't have become the woman who could return and finally offer something lasting. I had been waiting to feel that understanding: to have my need for distance, exploration, and sovereignty seen as reasonable. To have my response recognized as strength—not separation.

It had felt like no one truly got it except Gabe. But now I could finally see where I hadn't *let them in*. Because I hadn't fully known what I was doing myself, not until now. So much had been buried, not for dismissal, but for *survival*.

I thought of Rhea in our final meeting, when she said:

"If I wasn't like this, I think I would die."

But we had lived.

And we could go a new way.

JULY, 2021: SOUTH CAROLINA

TWO TRAINS IN THE NIGHT

I looked out the window.

We were passing Charleston, a single light hanging over the sign. The train car was dark, as this was the overnight portion of the trip. Somehow everyone around me was asleep.

Mom sat next to me, snoring softly, her breath coming in and out in little clicks. I couldn't find that rest myself. The seat was just as stiff as I remembered, but more than that, I felt too alert after a week of packing boxes, shipping them out, wrapping frames, and folding up clothes.

Moving was familiar by now; I had done it about seven times in the last five years.

The big, exciting move from Chicago to the West Coast. Then the heavy, sorrowful moves for myself and behalf of Gabe, from LA and Miami back to Long Island. Then there was the two-month attempt to relocate from Long Island to Chicago, and back again.

But this time was different. This time, I wasn't storing things while unsure of their future relevance. I wasn't reacting to tragedy. I wasn't frantically throwing everything in the car and counting the days until I could collapse. I wasn't packing up the remnants of an old life.

I was building the foundation of a new one.

Unbelievable, even to me, I was back on the dreaded auto train —the one I had declared I would never step foot on again—headed to the infamous state of Florida. A place where I thought life ended. I had heard the true call of it in that bathtub in Chicago last autumn.

Once the case wraps up, the next stop will be Florida again.

When I received the message, I felt the telltale softening in my body; the quiet simplicity of its truth, even in my resistance.

I didn't know what came much further than this first step.

But I knew it was a start. Crazy, but right.

Once I surrendered to the idea that I was somehow being called to this state, a specific location kept surfacing in my mind:

St. Petersburg. A small, quirky city near Tampa.

I kept hearing its name again and again, like a little spinning wheel on my morning walks. It was on the west coast of Florida, just a few hours from Miami.

Gabe had actually texted me about the area a couple years earlier, when he had visited there:

> What if we all moved to the West Coast of FL? Beaches are incredible here.

> I love the idea for you, but I'm a Cali girl now :)

Yeah, I don't even know why I bothered
asking ALIBU!

ALIBU. That had been his new nickname for me when I moved
to LA. It was like the Venice-Beach-themed WWF wrestler from
the '80s—*MALIBU*—but without the M, to make it even closer to
my name. The more wild and bleached my hair became from the
ocean, the funnier we found this.

Soon, the idea of St. Pete being a new home became stronger,
as I realized that I actually had the anchor of community there.
There was Aubrey, Celeste's daughter and more family than friend,
who lived in nearby Tampa with her husband and young children,
who I was excited to have quality time with. She was Gabe's age,
and we had grown up together choreographing dance shows for
our parents, celebrating Fourth of July, and driving around Huntington listening to hip hop during visits home.

Then there was Maureen, Gabe's high school girlfriend and
one of my all-time favorites. She brought just the right touch of
mischief into my teen years, like sneaking me into my first bar,
while always watching out for me once we were inside. We had
stayed in touch ever since. As an adult, she had made a lovely
home in St. Pete, founding an ocean-sourced sea salt company.

Both Aubrey and Maureen had remained beloved family
connections, and I was looking forward to the time and space to
be together in this chapter, too.

That same week, I called my friend Nia to ask where she had
decided to move, since I knew she was leaving LA. She answered
from the road—and to my surprise, explained she was in the
middle of driving from California to Florida, with her final desti-
nation being *St. Pete.*

"Something's calling me there," she said. "It's the sunniest city
in America, so I'm checking it out!"

As it turned out, our friend Gosia had already made the leap a
few months earlier. As if in some invisible spiritual caravan, we

had all gone from Chicago to LA—and now, it seemed, to Florida. I had always loved living in the same place with them: deep conversations, plenty of laughter, and the ease of just being together.

So I booked a flight to check it out.

Nia picked me up from the airport with her rescue dog, a wide-eyed little Chihuahua mix named Pugsley. As she drove me through the city, I thought:

Oh. Now I get it.

The city felt like a fusion of the places I'd loved before. Short buildings covered in street art and quirky local businesses, like Portland. Palm trees, the ocean, and a slow-moving vibe, like Venice. And friendly, conversational people, like Chicago.

Pugsley hadn't barked once in the nearly two years since Nia adopted him; we used to joke he'd taken a vow of silence in this lifetime. But he surprised us both by barking the moment I walked into their apartment.

"He wants you to know you're home!" Nia laughed.

Maybe this could be home, I thought.

We took the elevator up eighteen floors to the rooftop deck, where an electric-blue pool shimmered under the late afternoon sky. Woven lounge chairs circled the water, surrounded by festive people watching the Grand Prix car race on the street below. An intricate track had been set up around the building and out toward the waterfront. I hadn't known it was Grand Prix weekend when I booked the trip, but this building was known for its perfect view of the race—people waited all year for an invite up to the roof. I thought back to Mom and me dodging race car drivers on our road trip, and felt confident I much preferred this vantage point.

Clouds of lavender, pink, and coral stretched across the sky. As awe-inspiring as Venice Beach skies had been, this was a different version of beauty. Instead of watching the sun drop into the ocean, I watched it melt behind a skyscraper. And in the morning, it would rise in blazing glory over the vast blue bay. The view felt like nostalgia colliding with something brand new.

I hadn't lived anywhere quite like this before. But for a couple of months in Miami, Gabe had. Like so much else in these last few years, could I pick up where he left off?

I laid back in one of the lounge chairs and thought,

This is the building for me.

But as strong as the desire was, it also felt impossible. It seemed like a lot more people besides us had gotten the hit to move to St. Petersburg, FL, since the pandemic began. Every apartment building I called was booked solid with tenants for the next year, if not two.

A couple of days later, Maureen, Nia, and I headed down to St. Pete Beach, a fifteen-minute ride from downtown. It was a Friday around lunchtime when we arrived at a colorful little beach bar called Bongos, where live music played and everyone looked like they were on vacation, having the time of their lives. We poured piña coladas from the bar into Yeti thermoses and floated in the warm, turquoise ocean, dissolving into giggles over everything and nothing in particular.

During the course of my visit, I found that St. Pete felt like a city on permanent 90s-style *MTV Spring Break*—but with yoga studios, coffee shops and unique art museums layered in. I was immediately drawn to them: The James Museum of Western and Frontier Art, The Salvador Dalí Museum, and The Imagine Museum, where everything was made of glass.

There's a spiritual teaching that states that *The opposite of being a victim is becoming a creator.* I was ready to reclaim my creativity and remember the spark of inspiration inside. I started painting again and reading Gabe's copy of *The Artist's Way.*

That fun beach hang was also my last full day on this St. Pete visit. Eventually, I floated back to shore and sat alone with the water up to my neck as I began to open The Records—just like I had on my final day visiting Gabe in Miami.

But this time, I wasn't advised to brace myself for what was next. Instead, The Akasha told me:

The perfect apartment in St. Pete will be ready for you next month.
It's a one-bedroom in the building you want.
Don't talk yourself out of what's yours.
Let yourself have it.

And it was. And I did.

I even flew back once more to meet the leasing office in person and make sure it was all in place. I was okay with doing things that seemed a little unreasonable when I felt the truth of this—because, as it turned out, life itself tended to be a little unreasonable, too

After I officially signed the lease, I stepped out of the chilled, perfumed air of the renting office and walked out the sliding glass doors towards the St. Petersburg Pier. After the cold seasons in Chicago and New York, I wasn't used to the Florida spring heat anymore. By the time I had made the 20-minute walk, I was grateful to hop on the little white trolley that drove up and down the pier, picking up overheated visitors.

I pulled myself on and sat down. As we rode down the landscaped path, the instant breeze was refreshing. The water was so vast and so blue, and I even saw a couple of dolphins flip by. It was gorgeous. And I was going to let myself have it, just because.

As the pleasure of the moment hit me, I began to quietly weep. My face flushed pink, streaked with hot tears, and I thought

Dad should be here.

He would love this place so much that I could almost see him on my new balcony, jamming on his guitar. Dad had poured so much of himself into loving his people, working hard and making music, holding it all with heart and devotion. And he didn't get to be here for the fruits of that labor; to make plans with Mom for the next stage of their life together.

And Gabe. This had been *his* fresh start before mine, and it still should be. I wished with everything I had that I could call him; could schedule a visit from his side of Florida to mine, and laugh at our luck at being in the same state, for however long it would be right to stay.

And yet, even with the "shoulds" that grief always brings, and the great waves of sorrow washing over me, there was nothing to change. Nothing I could change. I needed to welcome the ache that would be waiting on the other side of every joyful milestone.

It would **all** have to be welcome now, if I was ever going to open the door and let a new life inside.

I had carried this memory and realization when I flew back to Long Island to start getting ready for the move. Now the day was finally here.

I lay back in my seat on the dark, quiet train and thought about all the boxes on their way to my new apartment. Some were mine, and some were Gabe's, like his kitchen supplies, his books and crystals, and a small glass bottle of his ashes that I would put in a place of reverence in the new apartment.

Next weekend, April was driving in from Miami and bringing Gabe's favorite gray and white woven chairs from the storage unit —the ones he'd kept on his balcony. And the matching *WAKANDA FOREVER* tea mugs.

I was buying some things, too—deeply feminine, soft-to-the-touch items in shades of gold, pink, and white. This was a completely foreign colorscape to the old me. Just last month, I had chosen the first pieces of new furniture I'd ever bought: a cozy cream-colored couch and loveseat in a mid-century modern style, to be delivered the week I moved in.

The experience of having a place that was just mine was about to begin. Who was I as a householder, and what did I *really* like in a home? Through the sea of apartments I had shared with room-mates and boyfriends, I had never fully asked myself this before. But now, I had loosened up on the rules and identities that once took priority over my own care and delight.

My work was also coming along, this time fully interwoven

with my wellbeing, as I had intended when making that first big move to California five years earlier. My client practice had slowly been rebuilding itself since the previous spring. Even during this bizarro interlude when nearly everything else was in fact on hold, many people were realizing this was at least a time they could turn inward and do some self-reflective healing—maybe in addition to learning how to make sourdough.

With the consistent support of my therapist Karin, I felt steady and available to hold a small circle of clients who were ready to dive deep during this new opening of time. What I also found was that the work I was facilitating was rooted in the same values, but carried something new. It had a different weight, a deeper gravity. I now knew for certain: we cannot outrun what is ours to experience.

My father's passing had first initiated me into this path, and I had thought every step since then had moved me farther away from being caught off guard by life. But the most shocking and disorienting parts had came later—not before my spiritual practice, but years into it, after all the big "breakthroughs."

And thank goodness for that. It was how I survived, how I alchemized pain into strength. How I came to know who I truly was, and why I was really here. I no longer saw the process as a sharp before-and-after, but as an integration of then and now.

With the revelations of these recent years came a deeper acceptance of the challenges my clients brought to me. I began to see that my role was no longer to shield them from pain, or for the Akashic field to stop what was part of their greater journey. The magic of the story beneath the story was in trusting them to live it out, to receive the gifts and the power that comes from the full experience.

More than ever, I was walking with my clients, alongside them in their experiences, instead of feeling responsible to change the course of what was happening. Success and desired outcomes could still find them, at the right time and place. The Akashic energy was there for their highlights and joy as well as the pain that was waiting to be felt and understood. There was no need to rush.

I also began developing new virtual group sessions focused on disappointment and endings—because these were the topics I had the most fresh, active insight into. It was my current reality. And to my surprise, people wanted to attend. The pandemic years had initiated many of us into such topics. These circles became a place to connect, to create value and meaning. The conversations were raw but ultimately uplifting. There was freedom and healing in simply being with what was true.

This shift in understanding opened doors to a kind of work I hadn't fully anticipated: becoming a medicine holder for grief. It shattered the old assumption I carried that people might find me too sad to work with. I had worried that in my current way of being I was too much to host for a visit or to invite to a birthday dinner. And yet, here were people who wanted to pay me for my time and presence—with full awareness of what I had endured and what I was still moving through.

Clients reflected that my access to deep grief was actually one of the most supportive gifts I had to offer. They had come to me for a different pressing reason: relationship struggles, business development, or curiosity about the Akashic Records. Yet in many sessions, a deeper thread emerged—the need to be with grief.

Sometimes it was a past loss, a chapter with family, work, or relationships they hadn't realized still needed tending. Other times, it was an unexpected death close to them, one they hadn't known was coming when we first began our work together. And of course, there was the collective grief of the pandemic—its illness, isolation, and near-constant stories of loss. If they were drawn to me during this time, it often meant they, too, were entering a grieving journey of their own. As several clients told me at the end of our programs, working with someone who had experience inside that space helped them find their footing.

This experience taught me something invaluable: grief doesn't diminish our ability to share our gifts. We still have so much to offer, even in sorrow, as long as we're honest about our capacity and willing to seek solid support. In fact, when someone has truly touched and integrated real loss, they have *more* to share, not less.

That honesty became a cornerstone of my work during this season and beyond. I was navigating the hardest chapter of my life, yet for the right people, my presence in its raw and unvarnished form was exactly what the process called for. They found me in unexpected, organic ways. I wasn't marketing or broadcasting my availability; I posted the occasional video, stayed in touch with parts of my network, and shared sparingly on social media. Clients arrived through referrals or a spark of recognition from a post or transmission. What drew them was the sense that I had built something steady and rooted over the last decade. It didn't require me to pretend I was someone I wasn't, to wait until this chapter was "over," or to reverse back to the way things had been before.

I had been forever changed—and so had the way I showed up.

I checked the time as the train rattled toward the next stop. 3:30 a.m. In just a few hours, we'd roll into Florida, the hot sun beginning to climb the horizon. We'd pick up the car, and Mom and I would stop for a big breakfast: eggs, blueberry pancakes, bacon, fruit, plenty of coffee and tea. Then came the final short drive to St. Petersburg. To my new home.

I glanced down at my phone. A photo memory had popped up from the "on this day" feature. It was a blur of trees outside a train window. The same train window I was looking out of now. I stared, stunned. I'd thought it strange enough to be back on this train at all, but hadn't realized: it was exactly two years *to the day* since I'd last taken this trip when I was hauling everything back from Miami after Gabe.

Two years already. Only two years. That stretch of uncertainty, isolation, and despair had once felt endless. Like I would never escape. Like I would have no future. Like I would never care about anything again.

And yet, here I was caring again. Picking out a new coffee table and feeling excited about the swimming pool.

Of course, my heart remained more broken than not. Missing my brother still occupied much of my thoughts and shaded many of my experiences. To keep my system from rattling, I needed life to remain small, slow, enclosed, soft. I probably would for a long time, no matter how much my ego insisted on being ready for fast, open, productive, big. That part of me still clamored over time lost and all the things it believed needed to happen ASAP. For me. For Gabe.

But in my own way, I was moving forward.

I could move forward because even in this pain and uncertainty, I trusted myself. I was willing to meet myself in any situation. I now knew who I was in the deepest of suffering, the greatest of disappointment, and the darkest of grief.

Gabe used to say that if we really wanted to know ourselves, the most important question to answer was:

"Who am I when I don't get what I want?"

It's easy to be patient and grateful when things are going our way. But who are we when they don't? When it doesn't work out like we thought it should? How do we respond? How do we treat others and ourselves?

While in the midst of integration, I was coming to know who I was when I didn't get what I wanted. And for the most part, I liked that woman. I trusted her heart, her skill, and her resilience.

What I knew for sure now was this: I was still available to love and be loved, even if it looked different than before. I could still offer meaningful, authentic service to others. I could allow the tests of this tragic time to take new forms. I could notice the humor and beauty again—and I was laughing more. I knew where I had stumbled: where I had trusted what wasn't trustworthy, acted out, or held resentment instead of speaking my needs clearly. And I could hold compassion for my past without needing to deny or repair it.

There was still so much unanswered and unknown, still parts I was praying to heal. I thought back to the letter I had written to Gabe for the cremation ceremony, to the promises I had made.

I have to get bigger now. I will honor and care for myself and our family. When there is a choice to be generous, I will choose it, like you always did. I will let your love and wisdom flow through me.

That commitment still burned inside me, and holding onto it would guide me where I was meant to go. I had to learn to live beyond my brother's life. To let myself meet and even fall in love with people, places, and things that would never know Gabe. But maybe, through me, they could. Maybe they would love him, too.

Getting on this train was a decision to trust where our history and my future were bringing me. My lineage, my family, my home, and the old ways that would ultimately be surrendered. The me working on my laptop in the tent and breaking into a moldy apartment for my suitcase. Sitting in the hospital room holding Bubbie's hand, and listening to Dad's music in the car. Saying goodbye to Gabe at the funeral home. Walking out of the lawyer's office and then the doctor's office. Carrying heavy boxes and heavier stories.

The me crying to her big brother, and the me crying for her big brother. The me at the essence of *Dark Times Catering*—laughing in a restaurant with Mom and our people, playing music, setting down the photos and the candles next to the plates of food, honoring our dead and nourishing the living.

All of these parts, they would come with me as I moved onward. They would be interwoven into every decision, every experience, every brave new thing.

I looked down at my phone again. The photo of the same train window going in the opposite direction was still there. I pressed the side button, and the screen faded to black.

The memory of that trip and the reality of this one became two trains passing in the night,

One the whisper of an ending never to be forgotten.
The other barreling toward the beginning of whatever came next.

Acknowledgements & Gratitude

The journey of *Dark Times Catering* was supported by an incredible village, and I offer my heartfelt appreciation to everyone who helped bring this project to life.

Lizzie Appel, my memoir writing advisor: With such gratitude, thank you for your steady guidance and creative nurturing. This process has been a profound gift and an era I will never forget. You carried the vision with humor, expertise, and compassion. My life and writing have been changed by your support.

Allison Yeh, my editor: Your discerning eye gave this book clarity, precision, and strength. Thank you.

To my beta readers: Celeste, Amanda, Sara, Susan, Vanessa, Matt, James, and Erin. You gave the generous gift of time, focus, and encouragement when this was still a raw story in a Google Doc. You helped me see this was a book meant to be shared and opened my heart. My gratitude also extends to everyone who read segments and offered feedback and enthusiasm to move this project forward.

To everyone whose presence shaped the events of this book: Whether as family, friend, practitioner, or someone we met along the way, I am deeply grateful for your impact and for allowing me to tell a part of the story.

To the friends who reminded me joy is possible after loss: Your listening and care encouraged both the writing and my return to life. In particular: Aubrey, Susan, Sarah, Dylan, Jess, Nia, Mel, Arul, Maureen, Kevin, Vanessa, Lauren, James, Anna, Sean, Anne, Rhapsody, and Ali. Love and thanks to those here and beyond this page — I carry gratitude for each of you.

To my clients: It was a true honor to work with you during this unprecedented era. Your inspiring commitment to transformation embodied the healing wisdom and communal strength that can be found in grief's landscape. See you in the field...

To the practitioners: In the hardest season, you helped me find a way through, and I am forever grateful. Thank you for your support and expertise, and for allowing me to share part of that process.

To my family: The love, humor, and resilience that run through our story are woven into these pages. May we continue to heal and create together. In particular, thank you **Aunt Rosemary** for your unwavering belief and support, and **Uncle Marty** for your steady encouragement and care. And to the beloved ancestors, especially **Bubbie** and **Grandma**, who have held this journey in spirit. Thank you for the love and courage.

To my mother, Gina: *Wow*, what a journey we've had. With deepest gratitude, thank you for giving me the freedom to write about our hardest times and the trust to share what had long been private. Your strength is immeasurable, and your creative insight and editorial feedback elevated this book in powerful ways. *Dark Times Catering* holds a profound era of our relationship — one I am proud to have here to remind and inspire anyone who is meant to read it, including us. Love you, Mom!

To my father, Chuck, and my brother, Gabe: Your legendary compassion, bravery, and gifts for storytelling — and your shared devotion to making art of your lives — were the great inspiration behind this book. It is the privilege of a lifetime to share some of your essence and your stories here. May these pages be a space for those who knew and loved you to feel your presence once again, and for those who never had the chance, to come to know you now. Love you always.

And finally, to you, the reader: Thank you for stepping into our world, for letting it touch and change you, and for carrying this energy forward — to your own *Dark Times Catering* tables and into the lives you touch. I am rooting you on.

Love,
Alee

ABOUT THE AUTHOR

About the Author

Alee Reina Hoffman is an Akashic Records guide and healing artist who has held a professional practice for nearly two decades. She works with clients around the world to reveal the most powerful themes and storylines of their lives, and to find the beauty within it all.

You can find Alee on all social media platforms @aleereina. She has a special offering for readers of this book at aleereinahoffman.com.

For more about Alee's work and special offerings for readers
of this book, scan here.